PALGRAVE POCKET CONSULTANTS

Palgrave Pocket Consultants are concise, authoritative guides that provide actionable solutions to specific, high-level business problems that would otherwise drive you or your company to employ a consultant. Written for aspiring middle-to-senior managers working across business at any scale, they offer solutions to the most cutting-edge issues across modern business. Be your own expert and have the advice you need at your fingertips.

Available titles:

ATTRACTING AND RETAINING TALENT
Tim Baker

MYTH-BUSTING CHINA'S NUMBERS
Matthew Crabbe

RISKY BUSINESS IN CHINA
Jeremy Gordon

THE NEW CHINESE TRAVELER
Gary Bowerman

THE WORKPLACE COMMUNITY
Ian Gee and Matthew Hanwell

Forthcoming titles:

MANAGING ONLINE REPUTATION
Charlie Pownall

PUBLIC RELATIONS IN CHINA
David Wolf

CREATING A RESILIENT WORKFORCE
Ivan Robertson and Cary Cooper

Series ISBN 9781137396792

About the Author

Tine Huus, M.A., B.Sc., and B.Com., is a Dane living in Copenhagen. She has more than 25 years' experience within organization development, controlling, innovation management, change projects, business cases, scorecards, and metrics from FMCG, consultancy, and hi-tech industry. She has held management positions at Carlsberg, Nokia, Ramboll Group, and Nabisco Brands. She lived abroad for 15 years, in Finland, Ireland, and the UK. On a voluntary basis, she worked as a marketing officer, Information Technology Survey Group, a benchmarking organization for global hi-tech companies, and co-founded the International School of Dublin. She is the founder and CEO of Best Work of Our Lives, an international consultancy business within organization development, talent management, and employee engagement. She also teaches business economics and innovation management.

How to Use and Apply Human Capital Metrics in Your Company

People Data

Tine Huus

International OD Consultant, Founder and CEO, Best Work of Our Lives Ltd, Denmark

First published 2015 by
PALGRAVE MACMILLAN

Palgrave Macmillan in the UK is an imprint of Macmillan Publishers Limited, registered in England, company number 785998, of Houndmills, Basingstoke, Hampshire RG21 6XS.

Palgrave Macmillan in the US is a division of St Martin's Press LLC, 175 Fifth Avenue, New York, NY 10010.

Palgrave Macmillan is the global academic imprint of the above companies and has companies and representatives throughout the world.

Palgrave® and Macmillan® are registered trademarks in the United States, the United Kingdom, Europe and other countries.

ISBN 978–1–137–46694–5

This book is printed on paper suitable for recycling and made from fully managed and sustained forest sources. Logging, pulping and manufacturing processes are expected to conform to the environmental regulations of the country of origin.

A catalogue record for this book is available from the British Library.

A catalog record for this book is available from the Library of Congress.

Typeset by MPS Limited, Chennai, India.

Contents

Preface

When my network in London approached me for writing this book, I thought, why not? Even though metrics can be a hard topic to love and at times in my career I have wanted to explore people as opposed to number crunching and data analytics. For the last 15 years, I have worked for global companies and communicated in English. A Dane can stand up to the challenge of writing a pocket consultant book about metrics in English and at least I will not be competing with Karen Blixen!

I have a lot of experience with metrics. I am a humanist and economist so combining hermeneutics and mathematics has somehow become my destiny. As a controller and accountant, I worked with financial metrics and balance sheets. As a consultant, I worked with cost benefit analysis, balanced scorecards, and SWOTs. As a portfolio manager for internal venture businesses, I worked with innovation management, project management, and business plans with survival objectives. Almost ten years ago, I moved into Organization Development and became responsible for human capital metrics.

As a manager I have applied human capital metrics, though in my first manager roles, we did not talk about human capital and mostly managed salaries and other employee-related costs. Later, when recruiting new employees, we used test data and later again, performance evaluations, employee engagement ratings, and team and manager effectiveness measures.

We are yet to see a global standardized measurement framework and approach for people processes as we have for financial processes such as the IAS (International Accounting Standards) and IFRS (International Financial Reporting Standards). This should not deter us from scoping human capital metrics for our companies and becoming evidence-driven and analytical around people decisions. The scope of human capital metrics taken in this book is that they would cover the spectrum of talent management objectives in your business. I have used the Employee Life Cycle to ensure that all relevant talent decisions are covered by the metrics outlined.

This book is your pocket consultant on how to use and apply human capital metrics in your company. It starts out by defining what human capital and human capital metrics are and ends with possible calls to action. From a definition to a call to action is a long way and that journey is described in the chapters of the book in pragmatic terms and accompanied by examples, cases, frameworks, and tools. It is meant to be read front to back, however, if you are the impatient type, you could skip to Chapter 3, The Machine Room, or go directly to Chapter 5, A Toolbox for Managers. Or you could start with Chapter 8, Metrics for Skeptics, and then proceed in chronological order.

Finally, I would like to thank Wilson Wong for sponsoring me as a writer with the publisher and Ian Gee and Matthew Hanwell for being inspiring colleagues and true friends, having reviewed the book and coached me on towards its completion.

I dedicate this book to my father and mother, and Bo, my incredible partner in life, and Sif and Rolf, our two children.

chapter 1

Why Bother about Human Capital Metrics?

If we in business aspire to make better people decisions and take more targeted people actions, we must bother about human capital metrics. Whatever business you lead and manage, people objectives are essential. Whatever industry you compete in, the roles, responsibilities, skills, and expertise of managers and workers should be part of the business plan. Your business plan helps to secure funding for your enterprise; it gives the business a sense of purpose and direction, and, finally, people objectives and financial forecasts provide the business with targets to aim for and enable the business to monitor its progress. Using and applying people data swiftly and cleverly are about improving business performance.

In this chapter, you will be introduced to the terms of human capital, human capital metrics, people data, and a brief overview of their history. Next, you find an outline of the value proposition for human capital metrics, seen from the employer's as well as the employee's perspectives. A central question is how usage and application of people data can counterbalance, if not eliminate, biases and mistakes in human judgment. The process from data to action is important, as the end goal of human capital metrics should be action. Another question is around urgency and how urgent it is for you to start bothering about human capital metrics. In this book I argue that in the current VUCA (volatility, uncertainty, complexity, and ambiguity) times, it should become a matter of priority. VUCA puts time, cost, and decision quality pressures on people and businesses that can be alleviated by measurement and management of organization culture and capabilities. Finally, I put forward the idea of an analytical culture as differentiator, what the characteristics are of an analytical organization, and how it starts with you as an individual organization leader. Knowing your people challenges and due decisions, and being able to bring them to successful outcomes, can become your distinct competitive advantage as an organization and unique brand as a manager. Being metrics literate is also likely to help you future-proof your career in VUCA times.

Human capital and human capital metrics

The term "capital" has several meanings in business. Its meaning in this context is as a factor of production. "Human Capital" is one form of capital or factor of production, others being natural and physical capital. Natural capital is all natural resources like land, air and water. Physical capital is machinery, buildings, equipment and finance needed for the production of goods and services. Human capital can be defined as the skills, knowledge, and experience of an individual or population, viewed in terms of their value or cost to an organization[1]. "Human Capital Metrics" are data points, in various shapes and forms, quantitative and qualitative, which organizations and managers collect to measure and manage people processes in the same way as financial metrics are collected to guide decision-making, performance, and compliance. The terms human capital metrics and people data are used interchangeably throughout the book.

In stark contrast to the human in human capital, "human capital" management was practiced as early as 1750 by slave plantation owners in the West Indies. Slave owners developed an equivalence unit called "the prime field hand" against which slave workers were measured and managed. Values of "half hand" and "quarter hand" were aggregated to prime hands as a production capability metric of the plantation[2]. If nothing else, this book will aim to help rehabilitate the term.

People data or human capital metrics have been in focus in management literature and HR consultancy practice for decades. In the first decade of the 21st century, software tools to hold and process people data have also become more mature. Still, human capital metrics, analytics, and big data for people decisions and results do not seem to be taking off in the same way as metrics are being used for other business processes such as marketing, sales, supply chain, operations and finance. You may ponder why human capital metrics are not being utilized more widely. I have wondered why this is the case and I think that it is surprising that we in business are not that interested in people. We have the tendency to see people in terms of salary costs and "people" are historically viewed from a humanistic perspective, meaning we can try to subjectively understand them, however, we cannot objectively explain and categorize them. The general lack of utilization and application could mean that development of this area within your company poses a competitive advantage, both in terms of improving business performance and in terms of setting the standard for an organization's measurement capability and analytical culture.

Human capital metrics should not be mistaken for Human Resource (HR) statistics. HR statistics are basic data on the workforce and how efficient the HR function is in terms of servicing and supporting the business. Whereas HR statistics typically has a transactional reach, with HR as service provider, human capital metrics support the entire business agenda, strategically and operationally, with HR in a business-consulting role. Human capital metrics are broadly focused on all people decisions and results.

I would like to give you a word of warning here at the outset: a metric is just a data point. If the metric is not understood, interpreted in the context, shared, and acted on, it will never have any impact. Getting the balance between measurement and management right is imperative and some will say that the 80/20 rule applies—with 80% time and effort spent on managing and 20% on measuring. Another danger is that organizations spend a lot of time and money on developing tools and technology without at the same time in parallel developing the ability to use and apply the metrics in ways that will make a difference for the business.

The value proposition

Culture eats strategy for breakfast[3]. Many organization leaders appreciate that however motivating their vision of the future is and however brilliant the strategy, neither can be realized, if people—who make up the culture—do not support it. People amount to a minimum 30% of the cost base of a company and hence constitute a great asset. Even small improvements in people processes will have bottom-line impact. People unlike machines cannot be turned on and off at random but must sit in fitting roles and be motivated to contribute with passion, creativity, and that extraordinary performance when they are at work. This is the kind of work environment you want in your company. In addition, challenging conventional thinking on people as costs, as opposed to assets, is only apt in the 21st century, several centuries after the abolition of slavery from where the term "human capital," as illustrated, originated.

Unfortunately the majority of leaders do not know what they want with their leadership. According to the current Edelman Trust Barometer[4], an annual global study on trust in business, there is a leadership crisis and the largest ever gap between trust importance and trust performance in business and government since the study began in 2001. One of the recommendations in their 2014 report was for the CEO to become the Chief Engagement Officer, taking responsibility for establishing the context in which change will occur. We increasingly trust technical experts and "a person like yourself" more than top leadership. In general, employee engagement surveys show a substantial gap in perceptions between senior management and experts or workers on engaging leadership and culture of trust. Top of the house perceptions can be three times as favorable and simply out-of-touch with their own organization and people.

There is plenty of research that demonstrates the connection between human capital and organization success.[5] Research from Gallup Q12, an employee engagement survey business, illuminates financial benefits as well as health and well-being benefits to businesses. Highly engaged and committed employees create between 10 to 20% more financial benefits such as customer recommendation, profitability, and productivity than an average workforce. Highly engaged and committed employees also create superior organizational health outcomes, for example being less than 40% absent from work, involved in 50% fewer accidents, and having between 60 to 80% better physical and mental health than their average peers. We can boil the ingredients of an agile and healthy performance culture down to:

1. A work environment that is both externally and internally focused.
2. Teams where diversity, collaboration, and execution are characteristics.
3. Purposeful Leadership from the boardroom to the front lines.

And we should be tuned in for high engagement AND high performance which together give us the desirable organizational impact in the form of better team performance, better product or service quality, customer loyalty, individual and organizational health, bigger market share, business growth and sustainable profit.

As an experiment, take a measurement for your business performance and a measurement for people engagement and check how they interrelate. To get management's attention, I once produced a graphical illustration overlaying the company's share price and employee engagement index for a period of five years. The two graphs were almost on top of each other, though with the employee engagement graph as first mover on increases as well as decreases. Such a simple illustration of interrelationship will create a lot of debate, particularly on what drives what. Whether high engagement predicts performance or high performance drives engagement. While this is a chicken and egg dilemma, the interrelationship is indeed established and managers will begin to care more about the way they lead and manage people for organization success.

Today's talent comes with aspirations, expectations, and choices. Employees want and aspire to be part of and contribute in a high performance environment, full of energy and excitement, where they are fully utilized and can develop. Employees expect their company to engage in an ongoing dialogue on how it is to work here. If they do not like it here, they have choices. They may just do their job and nothing more. They may choose to be creative solely outside of work. They will opportunity network for themselves, not the company. They may vote with their feet and leave. In most cases, your top talent is most critical and will act quicker.

Combining art and science

Accenture, a global consulting company, has found that 40% of major decisions are based on the manager's gut, not on facts[6]. In the case of major people decisions, I would deem this percentage to be even higher, perhaps around 70%, based on my experience.

The problem with managers, of course, is that we are human. We have biases. A typical bias is the one described above. We over rely on our first thoughts, become overconfident, or give too much weight to past experiences. We also make mistakes. A common mistake is to pose the wrong question or to frame a problem poorly. I believe that as a manager you should always challenge yourself and your subordinates with different frames and reframe the problem in different ways and at various points all the way through the execution process.

Used wisely, human capital metrics counterbalance, if not eliminate, biases and mistakes in human judgment. Data and facts offer an objective perspective. Data is the best starter for quality dialogues and decisions, perhaps especially for difficult conversations and tough scenarios. Companies, small and large, hold a lot of data in HR systems, and with managers asking relevant people questions and requesting this data—in new forms—this has the potential to greatly enhance people management capabilities and make decisions for the workforce across the business data-driven. Software can crunch piles of information and look for patterns that are not immediately apparent. It may point to unimaginable correlations and counter-intuitive findings.

These would be the claims of advocates of "big data." It is a fact that currently a lot of investment is going into big data business systems and the focus of this book will also be to help you build the managerial capacity to take a stand on big data.

I believe the essence is to use a combination of art and science. Effective decision-makers acknowledge subjective and objective factors and mix intuitive and analytical thinking. On the one hand, you use your experience, draw on the company culture, put your knowledge to work, consult with your network, and collaborate with peers. On the other hand, you gather relevant data and facts and use and apply measurements and analytics. This combination will help you arrive at impactful decisions and better results as well as greatly reduce your dependence on luck for success (unless you are Irish).

Beyond data: training a probing mind

We have all witnessed the data overload situation. Private, public, and non-for-profit organizations alike excel in amassing data, reports, and recommendations which many times fail to answer the simple question "so what" and end up gathering dust on the shelf or in the cloud. Conversely, too little data may limit your scope and opportunity.

Even before we start to gather data, we need to go beyond data. By this I mean that we must train our minds to be curious and probing all the way. Curiosity will enable you to ask the right questions, reframe the problem, and challenge conventional thinking. The probing mind never settles. It continuously seeks to raise the bar, and it sees opportunity in every difficulty. There is a Japanese saying that you do not really understand something until you ask "Why," five times.

Using and applying a probing mind in deciding why data is needed in the first place, then exploring what data is most relevant, and finally how to operationalize it, this is your challenge—and a challenge for which inspiration and input can be found in this book.

The process from data to action

By now, I hope you are more convinced that using and applying human capital metrics would assist you in making more informed and impactful people decisions and in doing so help you make a positive contribution to your business. As mentioned, human capital metrics like any measurement data need to be brought to life. We are talking about the process from data to action. In its simplest form, this process consists of three steps:

1.   Understand and make sense for yourself/the leadership team
2.   Share and reach a common understanding across your organization/ team
3.   Identify, priorities and manage change actions.

Step one involves reflecting on the set of metrics at hand and possibly discussing it with your peers. You start to make sense of the data and think in terms of your response and action to be taken. What is this telling you, what is it not telling you? What is your initial reaction? How is your reaction after sleeping on it? What themes are appearing for action? Do different data inputs, e.g. numbers and verbal comments, tell the same or a different story? How does it fit with reality?

Step two comprises sharing the data findings and your reflections with your stakeholders. How are you going to share it? Should the general findings be shared with everyone in your organization and detailed findings discussed with the parties involved? How will you conduct the meeting? Do you need an outside facilitator? What are your objectives?

Step three involves identifying, prioritizing, and starting/monitoring actions. How do you maximize commitment? How do you get performance excellence? How do you instill a hunger for agility? How do you monitor action, closing done deals, initiating new actions? How do you keep it alive?

Data never changes anything by itself, but accompanied by action, it has the potential to change everything!

It is a matter of urgency

You may be thinking whether human capital metrics and people decisions are really that urgent. Why should I start now? We have managed perfectly well in the past without it!

If the arguments above on viewing people as assets, have shown a connection between human capital and organization success, and combining art and science in people decision have not been convincing, recent research on global human capital trends may bring more wood to the fire. Current global human capital challenges have been identified as improving leadership at all levels, redefining corporate learning, building passion and purpose, helping overwhelmed employees by simplifying the work environment, and delivering on people analytics and big data.[7]

We live in VUCA times where decisions are taken against the parameters of increasing volatility, uncertainty, complexity, and ambiguity. We are also witnessing continued explosion of mobile, social, and cloud computing and technology. As we are coming out of the recession, with talent beginning to move again, we must take advantage of VUCA and the technological disruption by being fully aware, equipped and analytical about our options and alternatives.

In summary, all businesses, not only large corporations, are competing in a global, complex, digital, knowledge-based setting where managers at all levels must understand how to attract, engage, challenge, develop, and retain people and what human capital is most valuable and/or critical now and in the near future. Knowing your people challenges and due decisions, and being able to bring them to successful outcomes, can become your distinct competitive advantage.

Analytical culture as differentiator

Plato said,

the unexamined life is not worth living

This goes for our work life as well as our life outside of work. It is perhaps a good mantra for companies pursuing and encouraging an analytical culture (see Box 1.1).

BOX 1.1   ELEMENTS AND CHARACTERISTICS OF AN ANALYTICAL CULTURE

Elements of an analytical culture are:

- *Agility*, as expressed by using logic to support ideas, demands of high quality, developing others, managing complexity and multiple tasks, identification of new opportunities
- *Transparency*, as expressed by searching for the truth, getting to root causes, valuing negative results as well as positive, making the tough calls, holding people accountable
- *Consensus*, as expressed by soliciting ideas, fostering teamwork, resolving conflict, reaching across organization boundaries

---

These elements of agility, transparency, and consensus are not easy to attain and sustain. You may not be able to think of many companies who possess these. If we look to industry, hi-tech would probably dominate. This is an industry where disruption, innovation, and collaboration have long been the norm in order to survive, whereas other industries, for example banking, are now facing eroding business models and need to adapt swiftly. In the VUCA world, an analytical culture may be the means to fight disruption.

An analytical culture is also attractive because it focuses on the right things at the right time and balances intuitive and analytical thinking. It turns information into insight and pursues the right outcome. It looks backwards as well as forwards. Is this finding a trend phenomenon, or is it driving or even predicting change?

Culture is all of us within the organization and your efforts as an analytical organization leader will be part of building the analytical culture in your company.

It starts with you

This book is intended as a primer on fundamental ideas that all organization leaders should understand about good human capital measurement and management. It aims to demystify and simplify the process of understanding and working with human capital metrics. It is not about big data systems, needing a university degree in statistics to be involved, sophisticated software tools or HR statistics. It is about the capabilities of identifying your business-specific and critical people challenges, starting to measure them and moving on to making data-supported, informed, and future-proof people decisions.

As an organization leader in your company, in a people manager role outside or inside HR, this book will enable you to:

- Acknowledge the importance of human capital metrics and people decisions for sustainable business performance (present chapter)
- Understand how human capital metrics support execution of your strategy and how they can be used to manage your talent (chapter 2)
- Become familiar with the principles behind human capital metrics and types of metrics, calculation and interpretation (chapter 3)
- Frame and determine what people data are most useful for your company (chapter 4)
- Apply the standard human capital metrics toolbox with eleven key metrics to cover problems and decisions across the employee life cycle (chapter 5)
- Take advantage of the process from data to action and learn about best practice within employee engagement (chapter 6)
- Appreciate limitations and remove obstacles in working with human capital metrics (chapter 7)

- Avoid ending up as a skeptic of metrics (chapter 8)
- Get ideas for how to start with measurement or evolve measurement and management in your company (chapter 9).

It starts and ends with you. As Albert Einstein stated:

> not everything can be counted, and not everything that can be counted counts

not everything can be counted, and not everything that can be counted counts

chapter 2

Working Strategically with Human Capital

A good way to compete is to aim to be unique. Competition is not about being the best with a few winners and many losers. It is about being unique in the eyes of the customers you serve. A BMW is a good car and so is a Volkswagen. They can both be described as the "best" car, however, the question is which car is unique to you as a customer.[1] Human capital metrics can help identify that uniqueness inside your company and support execution of your business strategy. Human capital measurement has the potential to become talent management. In this chapter, several case examples help to illustrate how human capital metrics should be driven by the business strategy and how proprietary metrics for your specific strategic choice can be created. Working strategically with human capital also involves considerations about uniqueness, quality, access, privacy, and governance of people data. Usage and application of human capital metrics are dependent on the organization maturity of your company and will evolve with past experience and over time. You may want to look at the maturity matrix that I will introduce later in this chapter as an opportunity to progress from one level to the next at your chosen speed. Though this book promotes "human" in human capital over "capital," several of the measurement yardsticks we apply to people draw on concepts from economics weighing up both benefits and costs. At the end of the chapter, a summary of some of the benefits of working strategically with people can be found.

How human capital metrics can support your business strategy

Most companies have a people strategy as part of their overall business strategy. If you have a people strategy, it will most likely contain strategic people priorities or people levers for executing the business strategy of the company.

Let us focus on a case example. In our case company, a new leadership team has recently come in and established a new overall business strategy. The people part of the strategy remains unchanged on a high level, as the previously identified areas are still very relevant and under execution across the global business. The people strategy involves three priorities, which are leadership, engagement, and diversity. The leadership lever is targeting developing leaders on all levels of the organization in accordance with a common high-caliber leadership model. The engagement lever is aimed at creating a highly engaged and high-performing work environment. The diversity part focuses on a diverse, respectful, and inclusive way of working and collaborating.

As part of the new strategy, however, the leadership team has come to realize that, though the leadership priority should remain, the underlying leadership approach needs to be tweaked and refocused to better match the new business direction and deliver unique business results more rapidly. In brief, leaders need to be challengers and become role models of a challenger culture. A refreshed leadership model with the desired competencies and required behaviors is designed, tested, and implemented. The implementation is a matter of urgency and, therefore, requires regular and frequent monitoring of progress. Two human capital metrics are put in place to follow-up on and guide implementation:

- The first is a measure of how visible the culture change is to employees. Do they understand why this is important? Are the shifts in how things are executed happening? Is decision-making transparent and rapid, and are people being held accountable for high performance?
- The second metric is a measure of how leaders are being perceived as adapters and role models of the challenger behaviors.
- A quick survey, checking the pulse of the organization, is selected as the vehicle to collect data. The pulse check is mandatory for the entire company and contains company-wide questions. It takes place quarterly and reports are delivered to leaders with more than five responding subordinates.
- Results are rolled up from teams to departments to divisions to Profit & Loss (P&L) business units. Reporting shows quarter-by-quarter progress and difference to external and internal benchmarks.
- Targets are set, end of year one: 70% of employees should be positive on the indices, and, end of year two, 90% of employees should be positive. Leaders and teams with scores above target are identified and get a personal greeting from the CEO. Resources are directed to leaders and teams struggling.

To recap, this is an example of operationalizing a strategic people priority and working with human capital metrics strategically and operationally. Outcomes of the process were acknowledged to be a heightened sense of urgency, fewer leaders and employees sitting on the fence (the neutral group of respondents diminished quickly), and a shared understanding of change rationale and the new way of leading and collaborating.

People data considerations

Data is at the core of working with metrics, so let us now have a look at some fundamental considerations around management of people data:

- Uniqueness—how you exploit proprietary data
- Quality—how you can rely on it

- Access—how you get to it and how you can act on it
- Privacy—how you safeguard it
- Governance—how you maintain and store it.

Uniqueness

With respect to uniqueness, the above case is an example of unique or "proprietary" human capital metrics. The case company designed and developed bespoke questions, indices, and targets to serve their specific purpose. Though the approach may not be overly sophisticated, it can be defined as proprietary. It was implemented in a similar manner across the global business without localization of any form. English was the language offered to all types of employees alike. A proprietary performance measure as in the example can lead to improved decision-making and set you apart from other companies. Any organization can design its own metrics. Any organization can also start identifying data and data combinations that it alone possesses and will give you, if only temporarily, a competitive advantage. In addition, looking to how other industries use metrics and applying this at your company will create value and differentiate your company from others.

Data quality

It goes without saying that data quality is important. Data quality is an essential characteristic that determines the reliability of data for making decisions. IBM defines high-quality data as complete, accurate, available, and timely.[2] Complete data means the grouping and linking of all relevant data to a given employee. Inaccurate data due to misspellings, typos, and random abbreviations poses a huge problem for most companies. Available data involves accessibility on demand; you simply have the required data at your fingertips. Your people data needs to be timely, up-to-date, and readily available to support your decisions. Accordingly, to move forward with big data, IBM stipulates for organization leaders to begin by putting in place a strong foundation for managing data quality with best-in-class data quality practices and tools.

People data access

Data access is about your physical access to the information as well as its readability and actionableness. Physical access means how data is shared with organization leaders. This will depend on personal preferences and organizational communications approach. Leaders can get access in an email with link to data reports or data reports can be stored in intranet or shared drives. Physical access also means the length of time leaders have access. Typically, people data can be accessed for the current business year, in the same way as financial data, and comparison to previous years would typically cover three years of history. If your personal preference is to be able to access data beyond these limits, you should save this data locally. Data access is also about readability and actionableness. People information must be easy to get to, easy to understand, and easy to take action on. Ease of use and turning data into action are topics that will be dealt with throughout this book.

Privacy

Individual country laws regulate data privacy and if you operate in several countries, you need to check compliance and design your master data structures and people data processes so that they are generally applicable across your operations globally. A country's data protection act gives various rights to individuals with regard to the personal data that organizations hold about them, for example, a right of access to a copy of the information comprised in their personal data. People data is collected on the individual. For some people processes, such as performance management, the individual is the reporting unit and strictly governed by data protection regulation. For other people processes, such as employee engagement, data is also collected from individual employees, however, it is not stored for and linked to individuals but aggregated for reporting units such as a team, a business unit, or a country. Employees are given a confidentiality promise that they cannot and will not be identified by individual scores and comments and the organization has to safeguard this confidentiality promise through proper processes, tools, and guidelines.

Data governance

I believe that ensuring that an organization has good data is everyone's responsibility. This is true in the sense that everyone must take an interest in challenging and monitoring data quality. In most organizations, the operational responsibility for people data management is divided between the Human Resources function and the Information Technology function. HR defines what data is needed, how it is captured, and how it is maintained, while IT selects and runs, often with outside suppliers, databases and tools.

It is a mistake to underestimate data management efforts. Reliable and relevant people data is the starting point for reliable and relevant people decisions.

Usage and application depend on organization maturity

When looking to implement human capital metrics, organizations are likely to have different starting points, different external and internal pressures, different time horizons, and different investment needs and wants. For these reasons, organizations will find themselves at different maturity levels, whether on purpose or by accident. The matrix in Table 2.1 helps to cast light on different maturity levels, corresponding organization characteristics, and typical approaches to human capital metrics at each level of maturity.

To avoid complexity, the maturity matrix is limited to three stages. In reality there will probably be more destinations on the journey. You may find that your company is in-between levels or on one level within one area and on another level within another area. Not all companies need to

Table 2.1 Maturity matrix where organization maturity drives usage and application of human capital metrics

Maturity Level	Characteristics	Impact on Human Capital Metrics
Level 1: Immature. The company is generally immature in its approach to human capital metrics. There may be some localized usage.	Human capital metrics are met with suspicion. Limited understanding and acceptance of the value of working with people data and fact-based people decisions. The prevailing attitude is likely to be that this is HR statistics to be used by the HR function. There may be pockets of local business usage within the organization.	Poor data. Lack of leadership focus and interest.
Level 2: Aspirational. The company uses human capital metrics in selected processes. There is an aspiration to do more.	Human capital metrics are used in selected processes, e.g. performance management. Usage may be quite schematic with a focus on how to comply with the process and entering the required data. Continuous business usage may be lacking.	Usable data for selected processes. Leadership is supportive. Communications of purpose, motivation, and guidance may be missing. The organization may have fragile, stand-alone metrics. Data is generated but not applied fully.
Level 3: Mature. The company is mature in its approach and moving towards mastery.	Human capital metrics originate from the people strategy and HR's commitments to the business on high-ROI (Return-On-Investment) people processes. Data cascade into the organization to support execution and performance. Leaders pull metrics for individual people decisions.	Consolidated, integrated, and unique data. Leadership is becoming as passionate about people data as financial numbers. Human capital metrics support critical people decisions and guide organization development actions.

be at maturity level three. Your ambition will largely depend on the talent challenges in your industry and global competition for specific talent.

I believe the maturity matrix provides you with an opportunity to progress from one level to the next stage. The main focus of stage one is efficiency. As you move towards stage two, you begin to focus on effectiveness. As you move towards stage three, you begin to focus on impact. Most mature organizations fire on all cylinders—efficiency, effectiveness, and impact.

Moving from level one to level two

What kind of action does it take to move from level one to level two and what kind of resistance can be expected?

Action may include:

- Linking human capital metrics to the strategy
- Purpose clearly communicated and promoted
- Leadership cascading selected people targets into the organization
- Identification of local best practice and application of this company-wide
- Conversations happening in management teams on people data requirements and business needs.

Resistance may involve:

- Leaders not buying into the purpose of human capital metrics
- People part of the strategy being misunderstood and not accepted
- People targets being a tiny fraction of performance/reward and, therefore, considered inferior compared to other business targets
- Being stuck in local best practice, since it is not invented here, it is deemed unusable
- The business case being questioned with no investment granted.

Moving from level two to level three

What kind of action does it take to move from level two to level three and what kind of resistance can be expected?

Action may include:

- Human capital metrics becoming fully aligned with strategy execution
- All key people processes being included in order of priority

- Leadership begins communicating people data alongside financial metrics
- People data being fully reliable
- Proprietary people data being developed
- Human capital metrics coming to constitute a natural part of business decision-making and drive organizational development.

Resistance may involve:

- Individuals continually questioning the value of human capital metrics
- Leaders not being able to work with the data
- Data impact perhaps being counterintuitive and breaking existing decision-making patterns
- Teams finding it hard to handle the change
- Guidance on purpose and usage being unclear or lacking
- Analytical capability may be perceived as developing too slow or too fast, deeming it insufficient for current and new challenges.

Drawing on concepts from economics

As referenced in the introduction, this book advocates people as assets, not merely as costs. So the "human" in human capital is more important than "capital." It is the "human" that makes this kind of capital unique! Many of the measurement yardsticks applied to people are borrowed from economics and they naturally weigh up both benefits and costs.

Imagine you are a European business, headquartered in Denmark, with operations across Europe and Russia as your biggest market. This could be some the key people challenges you are currently facing:

- Russia is our biggest market and talent is scarce. How committed are our employees in Russia currently?
- On boarding: bringing on board new talent is critical for innovation and excellence in execution. How many new employees are high performers within the first year of employment?

- Leadership is a strategic people lever. Leaders at Headquarters should lead the way. How many top-quartile ranked leaders do we have at HQ?
- How do we justify the costs of training programs? CFO says to CEO: "What happens when we train people and they leave?" CEO replies to CFO: "What happens when we don't train people and they stay?"

Concepts and constructs from economics such as statistics, accounting, segmentation, Return-On-Investment, benchmarking, cost-benefit and break-even analyses[3] will help find solutions to the people challenges above.

People challenge one: commitment in Russia

Russia is our biggest market and talent is scarce. How committed are our employees in Russia currently? You might have run an employee engagement survey recently and you may have employee turnover statistics for the country. From the employee engagement survey you will typically get a % favorable score and, more importantly, you may by means of statistical correlation analysis understand what drives engagement in Russia, so that you can tailor interventions to attract and retain employees. From your turnover data, you want to see how many staff voluntarily (and involuntarily) leave the company, in absolute numbers and percentages of total headcount, per month, per function (some functions may be more critical than others), grouped by managers and non-managers, and by high-performing/top talent leavers. Perhaps you also have some exit interview comments to guide you. Collecting all this data and making sense of it will give you a good insight into commitment in Russia and what should be changed to improve recruitment and retention.

People challenge two: productive new employees

On boarding is critical for innovation capability and fast excellence in execution. How many new employees are high performers within the first year of employment? As part of the performance management process, a chart of employees at different performance levels can be found. In this context, a new employee is defined as having been employed within the last year. You compare the number of high-performing new employees with all high performers. Is this percentage score good or bad? You may want to compare the percentage to a relevant benchmark; essentially, you want ›50% of your newly employed staff to be high performers. You could also apply a Return-On-Investment calculation by quantifying outputs from employees and using this profit measure as the nominator and adding costs of hiring, on boarding and salary and using this investment measure as denominator.

People challenge three: leadership at headquarters

Leadership is a strategic people lever. Leaders at Headquarters should lead the way and have a bigger proportion of leaders with a top-quartile ranking and no leaders with a bottom-quartile ranking (that cannot be explained by the business context) compared to the organization overall. As part of the employee engagement process or leadership assessment bench, you will have data in a manager quality index that you can group into quartiles to check how HQ leaders stack up. Relative to the company overall, there should be no leaders in the bottom 25% (unless explainable by factors in the business context) and a good number of HQ leaders should be in the top 25% segment – perhaps you target having half of HQ leaders here.

People challenge four: value of training

CFO says to CEO: "What happens when we train people and they leave?" CEO replies to CFO: "What happens when we don't train people and they stay?" How do we justify the costs of training programs? Suppose we need to train 50 employees. We want to calculate costs, benefits and break-even. The cost of the program is €500 per participant, in total €25,000. Like with other training program of this kind, we expect that it will raise the knowledge of the employee by at least

10% for 90% of the participants. We now agree that the value of the 10% increase in knowledge is greater than €1,000 per participant. Total benefits can be calculated as 50 × 0.90 × €1,000 = €45,000. Instead of calculating costs and benefits, you can simply look at the agreed value of minimum €1,000 per participant and find that it more than covers the training program cost of €500 per participant. When costs equal benefits, a training program breaks even. With benefits of €45,000 minus costs of €25,000, this particular training program is far above the break-even point.

Drawing on concepts from economics gives credibility to human capital metrics, as organization leaders are familiar with and approve of these constructs from other business processes. It helps towards demystifying people data and people analytics. It also helps getting attention, interest, and investment to people processes.

Efficiency + effectiveness + impact

We touched upon impact. Where should leaders and managers spend their efforts? Where should investment flow? What organization capability is most critical? What competences are core? Working with human capital metrics supports identification and prioritization of scarce resources, be it time, money, quality, competences, ways of working, values, or culture.

If you remember the case example from the beginning of this chapter, illustrating how human capital metrics operationalize the people strategy, you will recall the two metrics our case company used to help leaders and the entire organisation adopt and apply the refreshed leadership competences. The idea is that leaders drive the implementation of the change. Leaders needed to be challengers and become role models of a challenger culture. We can plainly name the two metrics: 1) visible culture change and 2) leaders as role models. How would these two metrics have the most impact? It was decided to hold top-of-the-house managers accountable for progress on the index for visible culture change and team managers accountable for progress on the index for leaders as role models. A manager may wear two hats, for example, that of leader of an entire P&L unit (top of house) as well as that of team leader for his or her direct subordinates. Managers with two hats had both indices as performance targets. Managers with either top-of-house responsibility, including strategic program managers, or team leadership responsibility had the relevant one of the two metrics as their performance target. Being a leader for an entire business or function means being accountable for bringing the whole organization with you. Being a team leader, you bring your team with you. The measurement approach is complementary and will impact on the full organization.

There is no need to worry at this stage about principles, types, and calculations behind human capital metrics. There will be plenty of detail to follow in the subsequent chapters, as we go into the machine room (Chapter 3) and open the standard toolbox of metrics for managers to cover their entire talent management responsibilities (Chapter 5).

Human capital measurement equals talent management

As we have seen from the strategic people challenges above, people data measurement is, in essence, managing your talent. You tackle issues around on boarding, development, commitment, leadership and culture.

Talent management may be perceived as a term from the core vocabulary of Human Resources. However, it stems from consulting.[4] If we define talent management as the broadest frame for which human capital metrics come into play, talent management can be broken down into:

• Recruiting talent
• On boarding talent
• Engaging talent

• Developing talent
• Leading and managing talent
• Rewarding talent
• Exciting talent.

This breakdown nicely follows the employee life cycle. We will use these buckets of talent management for outlining and detailing human capital metrics as we proceed.

Applying human capital metrics to manage your talent is easier (once it is up and running), more stress free, and less dependent on luck or chance. How do you know if people are in fitting roles? Of course, you can ask them. They may not want to tell you or they do not fully know themselves. Relevant metrics will complement your dialogues on the matter. Human capital metrics will also support you in dealing with mismatches, talent that no longer fits and needs to be moved on or out. What are your people risks? If you do not have a people strategy, company culture, and competencies framework, in words and measures, you will not be able to formulate people risks, let alone mitigate them. A part of valuing your talent is that you have regular performance and development conversations based on objective targets and inputs from a range of relevant representative sources.

Some talent is top talent. What is the difference between talent and top talent? Well, top talent is the people who according to the selected metrics framework are categorized as high historical performers and with high future potential. Letting the people, who are rated as top talent, know that they are in this segment is also part of valuing and managing your talent. And being prepared to treat people top talent a little differently if you want to keep them is essential, too.

What is the difference between talent and top talent?

In the chapters to come, we will go into detail with what human capital metrics to apply to manage talent along the employee life cycle.

Benefits of working strategically with human capital

As this chapter draws to an end, it will be useful to reiterate some of the benefits your company can reap by linking human capital metrics to the business strategy and, in operationalizing people data, ensuring that the trinity of efficiency, effectiveness, and impact is being measured and managed.

- When linked to your strategy, human capital metrics will speed-up and remove execution obstacles, such as change resistance and people sitting on the fence.
- A prerequisite for working with human capital metrics is that your people data is reliable, up-to-date, accessible, actionable, and in compliance with relevant privacy regulations.
- Proprietary human capital metrics that are unique to your company will give a competitive edge.
- Concepts from economics help to establish credibility and facilitate investment.
- Human capital metrics illuminate leading and lagging teams and business units.
- Human capital metrics support the entire talent management cycle from recruitment to exiting employees.
- Management of people risks becomes possible.
- Practice makes perfect. Good human capital metrics are the basis for improving decisions over time.
- Nothing stops you from starting today! Start targeted and small. Build data and analytics capabilities as you go.

chapter 3

The Machine Room

In this chapter, we will be approaching the machine room, or the inner workings, of human capital metrics. The machine room is hot and noisy, not calm and quiet, as you would expect. There may be health and safety issues, if you get bored, lose your way or fall into one of the machines. Be prepared to get your hands dirty and stay focused as we look at the principles behind human capital metrics, different types of metric, sample calculations, meaning of results, benchmarking and target setting, how to interpret and contextualize results, the interplay of quantitative and qualitative data, and different organizational approaches to collecting and sharing human capital metrics.

And do not panic—all the human capital metrics outlined in the various chapters of the book can also be found in the alphabetically ordered appendix list for easy reference. The list can be found at the back of the book.

Getting to grips with the principles behind human capital metrics

In the previous chapters we have determined that people can be categorized as your biggest asset (as well as cost for many companies). Second, highly engaged employees deliver extraordinary results, both in terms of financial results and in terms of organization health and wellbeing benefits. Lastly, that human capital metrics aid people decisions across the entire talent management process. This nicely sums up the guiding principles behind human capital metrics:

- It is possible to estimate and classify value of people as well as cost
- Fairness and quality in people decisions and investments generate organizational success
- People data reveals value, cost, fairness, and quality of people processes across the talent management life cycle
- Human capital metrics counterbalance, if not eliminate, biases and mistakes in human judgment.

While experts in the field[1] would agree on these guiding principles, we are yet to see a global standardized measurement framework and approach for people processes as we have for financial processes such as the IAS (International Accounting Standards) and IFRS (International Financial Reporting Standards). You would indeed be able to calculate employee goodwill from your employee engagement level and put it onto your balance sheet; however, this is not yet common or regulated according to my knowledge.

In 2005, the Corporate Leadership Council, in collaboration with the InfoHRM Group, now part of SuccessFactors, established a framework for human capital measurement, called "The Metrics Standard" which includes 200 core human capital measures divided into various Human Resources topic categories.[2] The Human Capital Management Institute uses a similar approach in their comprehensive Human Capital Metrics Handbook of over 600 workforce metrics, which was updated in 2013.[3] In this book, I use talent management as the overarching framework and key metrics follow the employee life cycle being grouped according to the respective sub-process within talent management, that is, from recruiting and on-boarding talent through engaging, developing, leading, managing and rewarding talent, to exiting talent. In business, we are familiar with the concept of Product Life Cycle, and I believe you will find the Employee Life Cycle easy to work with.

The absence of a common standard should not deter any of us from scoping the measurement processes and standards for our companies and agreeing on how human capital metrics will be defined, measured, and interpreted. We have talked about people data requirements in the previous chapter and these apply to the measurement standards as well. Metrics should be used consistently and consecutively across the business and be supported by pedagogical metrics interpretation guidance to avoid mistrust of data, reports, and analyses, delays in decision-making, actions taken not addressing the real problems, and, perhaps most importantly, missed opportunities. What does this metrics tell us about our performance? Is this a good or bad result? What does this metric not tell us about our performance? Where should we focus?

Metrics should be used consistently and consecutively across the business

If you are looking to buy a software tool to hold your human capital measures, as I write, I do not believe there is a software solution comprising the full talent management process. It is typical to have recruiting data in one tool, employee engagement data in another, and reward, pay and benefits in yet another. Generally, available software tools are aimed at users sitting in the central Human Resources group who have overall responsibility for people efficiency. On the other hand, over the last few years, there has been a steep rise in the number of professional players in the field of integrated talent management software, and, if you are in a situation where you can start from scratch, not being dependent on former investments, you will have a good choice of professional software packages.

Types of metrics

Understanding metrics types is a first step towards identifying what measures most appropriately fulfill your management needs. Knowing about metric types is also important for correctly interpreting measurements and rapidly moving forward to interventions. The below list defines the typical human capital metrics types you will encounter (Table 3.1).

Table 3.1   Overview of metric types and examples of each metric type

Metric Type	Measurement	Metric Examples
Rate	Percentage	• Turnover rate • New Hire % of High Performers
Ratio	Fraction	• Career Path Ratio • Operating profit per employee
Composition	Breakdown into parts, a number, percentage, or significance allocated to each part	• Termination reason breakdown • Tenure distribution
Index	Scale	• Employee Engagement index • Top talent Recommendation
Qualitative input	Unstructured qualitative data to be grouped into themes/categories or evaluated against a list of predefined criteria	• Free-text comments in survey • Employee photos of company values

We will now, in turn, review each metric type by adding to the examples in the right-hand side of the overview its application, description, calculation, a sample calculation, and usage. Some of these examples will be included in the human capital metrics toolbox with a handful of key measures which you as a manager will need to achieve people acumen across the employee life cycle. The toolbox can be found in Chapter 5.

Examples of rate metric types

Turnover rate

Application: turnover rate is broadly useful in monitoring how employees consider their "deal" with your company, how well you manage to retain people, and what constraints the turnover rate puts on your business.

Description: the number of employees who leave the company during the reporting period as a percentage of average headcount. The reporting period is typically a month or a year.

Calculation: terminated employees/average headcount * 100

Sample calculation: 10/100 * 100 = 10%

Usage: turnover rate measures the percentage of employees who voluntarily or involuntarily leave your company during the given period. As in the sample calculation, a result of 10% means that employees who have left amount to 10% of the total average workforce within the given time period.

A high turnover rate (defined as more than 20%) can have negative impact on the company related to costs, skills, knowledge and experience, performance, and customer service. Costs will include immediate replacement, recruitment of new employees, lost productivity in the interim, and missed customer interaction. When employees leave, they carry their skills, knowledge, and experience with them and, too often, companies do too little to secure proper knowledge management and handover between employees. Remaining employees often feel stressed and disappointed and become a further constraint on a high turnover rate.

A low turnover rate (less than 5%) is not desirable either. Low turnover may indicate (career) complacency, foster insularity, and lead to lack of innovation capacity, as employees with new and diverse skills are not recruited. There is the notion of good versus regrettable turnover. Some turnover will actually invigorate your company.

The average turnover rate helps you understand the overall rate at which employees are leaving. However, to take targeted action and remove disadvantageous constraints, you will want to understand what part of the turnover relates to voluntary termination or those employees who choose to leave your company and go somewhere else. Involuntary termination, that is employees the company let go, is often less interesting. You may also want to understand how many of your high performers choose to leave your company. What part of the deal are they unhappy about? Where are they going? If your overall turnover rate is 5%, but your high performer turnover rate is 10%, you are obviously bleeding talent and this is regrettable turnover. Your high performers are difficult to replace. Moreover, it is likely to take more than one employee to replace a high performer and there is always the risk that the replacement employee may turn out to be an average performer. As average turnover rates may hide very high and very low turnover in parts of the organization, look for turnover hot and cold spots. These spots can be geographical, functional, or demographical. Turnover rates vary by industry and roles, for example call centers versus Research & Development teams.

New hire % of high performers

Application: the percentage of newly hired employees in the high performance segment is an indicator of the effectiveness of the organization, managers, and teams with on boarding of new employees, the quality of induction programs, and how inclusive your organization is.

Description: the number of employees who are hired during the reporting period with a high performance rating as a percentage of all high performers in the company. The typical reporting period is bi-annually or annually.

Calculation: newly hired employees with high performance rating/all high performers * 100

Sample calculation: 25/125 * 100 = 20%

Usage: the percentage of new hires in the high performance segment measures how many newly hired employees become high performers in % of all high performers. In the sample calculation, the company hired 50 new employees during the given period and has an average headcount of 500 people. The high performer segment is about 25% across the company with 125 employees in this segment for the period. A result of 20% means that new hires constituted 20% of all high performers.

A high new hire % of high performers (more than 15% or new hire high performer % segment larger than all high performer % segment, in the example, 25/50*100 = 50% compared to company overall 25%) is generally positive for the company, with new employees quickly getting up-to-speed and delivering outstanding performance, speedily becoming brand ambassadors, and being inclined to stay with your company. A high score also reflects a positive inclusive work environment where managers and team members care for and respect newcomers. Employees quickly becoming high performers will put pressure on the organization to maintain focus on high levels of utilization, development, and manager coaching, at least in the short run.

A low new hire % of high performers (less than 10% or lower than new hires' proportion of average headcount, in the example 50 new hires out of 500 staff, 10%) may indicate poorly planned and/or executed on-boarding process, inadequate utilization of new resources, lost productivity, missed innovation, costly turnover of new hires, lower team performance, lack of supervision and feedback, and a distrustful and complacent culture. Performance feedback must include more than the hiring manager's rating, which will naturally be skewed towards more positive results for the new employee he or she hired!

Examples of ratio metric types

Career path ratio

Application: as there is little room at the top of pyramid-formed organizations (which is the shape of most businesses), career path ratio helps focus on a range of career possibilities and steers people in different directions, not only upwards, in their career progression.

Description: total promotions relative to total transfers, with "promotion" being an upward movement in the organization and "transfer" being a lateral movement.

Calculation: total promotions/total transfers

Sample calculation: 300/600 = 0.5

Usage: career path ratio shows the degree of upward movement versus lateral movement at your company or business division. The hierarchical organization has limited promotion capacity, however, almost unlimited transfer capacity. Transfers are a cost-effective way of building, motivating, and retaining your talent base. For many professional and executive roles, lateral movements offer transfers between headquarters and country organization, within the same corporate function, cross-functionally, such as from Finance to HR, from line manager role to program manager role and vice versa. Employees are given new, stimulating, and challenging roles with little increase in costs.

If your organization has a career path ratio close to 1, it means your company is practicing too many promotions or too few transfers. As a manager, this can also be an important measure. It will tell you how good a corporate citizen you are in terms of letting your high performers go to other functions or teams or whether you tend to hoard talent. Of course, it is in the interest of the whole company that talented employees can have their career wishes satisfied internally—and are not being forced to go externally to progress their career. All managers will benefit from letting talent roam free inside the company; they give some and they get some.

Operating profit per employee

Application: operating profit per employee is a generally applicable measure of workforce productivity and the impact of your talent management practices. Take care when drawing conclusions from this measure, as industries and markets vary. Even within the same industry or market, two businesses can generate the same level of profit, however, one company has invested in automated production and uses fewer people while the other may use more traditional production methods and more human capital.

Description: average operating profit (before tax, interest, and depreciation) per full-time employee.

Calculation: operating profit/full-time employees

Sample calculation: to make this sample calculation as close to reality as possible, it is based on a real-life example—The LEGO Group—with numbers from their Annual Report 2013[4]—

mDKK 8.336/11.755 = DKK 709.145 per employee (approximately €95.000)

Usage: operating profit per employee measures bottom-line financial productivity of the organization as generated collectively by individual employees. Profitable growth—that is top line sales and bottom-line profits—is in all employees' interest.

Higher profit per employee means greater opportunities for people to expand their careers and to make more money. All business leaders want to see operating profit per employee increase year-on-year indicating that the organization is growing the right way, profitable and sustainable. You could set a target for your organization to be in the 75th percentile (top 25%) of a relevant benchmark group, for example your industry, as higher profits per employee equates to higher productivity.

Higher productivity can, in turn, be attributed to innovative and well-executed talent management processes and overall organization effectiveness. In the presentation "Leading Edge Talent Management," Dr. John Sullivan, HR thought leader from the Silicon Valley, asks whether bold talent management increases profit. He compares operating profit per employee for Silicon Valley-based hi-tech industry (HP, IBM, Facebook, Microsoft, Google, and Apple), pointing out that it takes nearly 15 times more employees at IBM to produce the same level of profit as Apple.[5] It can, of course, be debated whether an excessively high operating profit per employee is desirable (except for owners and shareholders), as it may mean employees are being taken advantage of, having to run too fast and getting too little reward for their performance.

Examples of composition metric types

Termination reason breakdown

Application: this metric is essential for organizations that fight for scarce talent and need to understand, monitor, and act on reasons for employee departures.

Description: distribution of terminations during a reporting period by type and reason for termination.

Calculation: termination by termination reason/all terminations * 100

Sample calculation: It is given in Table 3.2.

Usage: the termination reason breakdown is a composite measure that gives you an overview of termination type and reasons for employee departures (Table 3.2). It is necessary to look at types of termination or employees who decide to leave a job on their own accord (voluntary termination) and employees whom you have had to let go (involuntary termination).

Reasons for employee departures will vary from industry to industry and geography to geography and it is important to track applicable reasons from the beginning in order for your company to be able to make the necessary changes quickly. If you have difficulties recruiting talent, you will want to re-circulate talent. For example, the five employees who in Table 3.2 have been dismissed because of worsened business conditions in one part of the business could be moved to another part of the business instead of being allowed to leave. Investigating terminations due to inadequate job performance may be interesting. Combined with voluntary departures due to working

Table 3.2   Termination type and reason breakdown

Termination by type/reason	Number	Breakdown
Involuntary termination	10	40%
– Inadequate job performance	3	30%
– Business conditions	5	50%
– Absenteeism	2	20%
Voluntary termination	15	60%
– Career opportunities	8	54%
– Working conditions	2	13%
– Manager relationship	5	33%
– Changes in personal circumstances	0	0%
Total terminations	25	100%

conditions, the involuntary terminations due to inadequate job performance may represent an opportunity for you to motivate and hold on to existing talent instead of having to recruit in a scarce talent market. Voluntary terminations due to manager relationship are another area for investigation. Is the quality of leadership up-to-the-job? Is it the same managers who repeatedly cause departures? How can managers best be supported on retention matters?

Voluntary and involuntary terminations carry different costs and productivity losses and require different involvement levels from the company. An organization with many involuntary terminations may want to examine possible process failures caused by the layoffs and dismissals to get the business to heal and back on track. An organization with numerous voluntary terminations may want to scrutinize employee engagement feedback to address possible weaknesses driving talent away to competition.

Tenure distribution

Application: this measure indicates the degree of diversity in your company and helps to balance the diversity of your workforce. It illuminates tenure imbalances and shifts over time.

Description: composition of headcount by tenure at the end of the reporting period.

Calculation: end of period headcount by tenure type/end of period headcount * 100

Sample calculation: 50 employees with < 1 year tenure/500 total headcount * 100 = 10%

Usage: tenure distribution shows how many employees you have in each tenure group. At a minimum, you will want to see how many short-tenured, mid-tenured, and longer-tenured employees you have. Ideally, your total workforce tenure composition would match the marketplace in which you compete and your employees will be thinking and acting like your customers. In today's talent pool, you have employees from five generations—traditionalists, the baby boomers, Gen X, Gen Y, and Gen Z.[6] People will both want and need to work for more years in the future so the ability to cater for tenure and age diversity will become more and more important for a business.

High levels of longer-tenured employees mean the organization has considerable experience and significant knowledge of work processes, culture, and history. Again, an overrepresentation of this segment may hinder innovation and transformation capabilities.

High levels of short-tenured employees may mean the organization is growing fast and has challenges sustaining performance. The development needs of short-tenured employees may revolve around on-boarding and process knowledge whereas the development needs of longer-tenured employees may focus on leadership, coaching, feedback, and updating of technical skills.

Examples of index metric types

Employee engagement index

Application: the employee engagement index is essential in understanding and acting on how employees feel about working for your company. It typically represents an equally weighted combination of outcome measures such as pride, recommendation, and commitment. No one can tell you to be proud to work for your company. Your pride is an outcome of how well the company manages to align you to its purpose and mission and enables you to do the best work you can.

Description: this index measures employees' discretionary effort and intention to stay with the organization. Organizations source data for this index from the responses to one or more questions from employee surveys.

Calculation: average of % favorable scores of question items in the index—(Q1 % favorable + Q2 % favorable + Q3 % favorable)/3

Sample calculation: (I am proud to work for my company 80% + I would highly recommend my company to a close friend or colleague as a great place to work 70% + I rarely think about looking for a new job with another company 60%)/3 = 70% favorable

Usage: employee engagement is measured using survey results. Typically, the survey questions used rely on the 5-point Likert response scale with options ranging from 1 (strongly disagree) to 5 (strongly agree). For reporting survey results strongly agree (5) and agree (4) responses are collapsed into % favorable. Different organizations use different sets of questions and methodologies for measuring employee engagement. In this context, the employee engagement index is defined as an outcome metric demonstrating employees' pride in working for their company, how likely they are to recommend their company as a great place to work, and intention to stay with their company, as you can see from the sample calculation above.

High levels of employee engagement (more than 70% favorable on the index) predict employees' willingness to go above and beyond and intend to stay with the organization. High levels of employee engagement on its own is not enough to sustain high performance over time. Engaged employees must be aligned and enabled to direct their efforts towards the right goals and best way of collaborating and innovating.

Low levels of employee engagement (less than 70% favorable in the index) indicate that there are organization barriers to high performance. Employees cannot give their best; they may be sitting on the fence, merely being content, or in the process of leaving the organization. This "zombie-like" atmosphere can be very contagious. Barriers to high performance should be understood and removed. What is causing the lack of engagement? What can be done to change it? What do other companies do? In later chapters, we will look at methodologies and approaches for identifying enablers and removing barriers to high engagement and high performance.

Top talent recommendation

Application: with top talent as your jewel asset, it is useful to determine how top talented classified employees feel about working for your company and whether, when all comes to all, they would recommend the company to a close friend or colleague as a great place to work.

Description: top talent recommendation hones in on how the top talent segment of your workforce perceives working for your company. The bottom-line is whether they can recommend it or not. Top talent can be defined as employees with a high performance rating combined with a high potential rating. Organizations typically use a performance-potential 9-grid model to indicate performance segments. A targeted talent performance distribution of your workforce could be 30/60/10, with 30% in the top segment, 60% in the middle segment, and 10% in the needing to improve segment.

Calculation: strongly agree + agree responses by top talent/all responses by top talent * 100 (on the question item "I would highly recommend my company to a close friend or colleague as a great place to work")

Sample calculation: (34 responses + 44 responses)/120 top talent responses = 65% favorable

Usage: top talent recommendation measures the percentage of top talented classified employees who responded with "strongly agree" or "agree" to the statement of recommendation. In the sample calculation, top talent recommendation is at 65% favorable. It is below the company average of 70% favorable indicated in the above sample calculation of an employee engagement index. For your top talent, you would probably set a higher benchmark than for your average employee population. Instead of having a target interval of +/- 70% favorable as in the above employee engagement index example, you would apply a target interval of +/- 90% favorable.

It is important that your top talent has more favorable perceptions of working for your company than the average employee population. You want to get the best out of your top talent. You want them to stay. Most importantly, you will use your top talent to attract other top talent to your company. If they are likely to recommend your company as a great place to work, they will be ambassadors in their professional circles and network as recruiters on the invisible job market where talent is not looking for a new job or even aware of your company, but may only be persuaded by your top talents' word-of-month recommendation.

It is, unfortunately, quite common to find that top talent perceptions are lower than the average employee population. First, your top talent is by nature more critical than the rest of the workforce. Second, though organizations put a lot of effort into performance and potential ratings, they often fail to communicate to managers how they need to treat top talent differently and what interventions and development opportunities are available. Ironically, individuals classified as top talents may never get to know their special status. No one communicates this to them. The information is stuck in the system, or deliberately not communicated for fear of creating an "exclusive" group of employees— setting expectations of favorable treatment and potentially demotivating employees who are not in this group! Measuring how top talent perceives working at your company will help cast light on possible process failures and cater for and accommodate your top talent.

Examples of qualitative input metric types

Free-text comments in survey

Application: free-text comments are most useful for organizations that are undergoing change, face disruption, or experience rapid growth. Qualitative input can be compared to "market" research with the market being the employees. Employees possess a lot of ideas for the different forms of innovation in business, e.g. process innovation where some part the process is improved to bring benefit; product innovation where new products are created or improvements to products suggested, or even paradigm innovation where major shifts in thinking cause change.

Description: free-text comments from employees focus on a few urgent topics or your must-win battles.

Calculation: a formula as such does not apply. However, you can group comments into themes/categories, either by asking employees to do it themselves after writing their comment or by using brainwork or software, e.g. sentiment analysis tools.

Sample calculation: as an example, many companies include an open question in your employee engagement survey or on your intranet, "Thinking about your work, what one thing would you suggest should be improved at our company." Then you ask employees to group their comments into themes such as customers, products, business processes, work environment, leadership, and company values. You can then track, delegate, and apply comments by theme. Comment can also be attributed to business units and demographic cuts such as females/males or longer-tenured/shorter-tenured staff.

Usage: the confidentiality of a survey process often encourages employees, especially the more introverted individuals, to give honest and candid written feedback. If an employee does not want to be anonymous, the person will simply put his or her name by the comment.

Employees providing comments are a great input source, as they are close to the customers, design and develop the products, use the business processes, collaborate with and are leaders, and make decisions within the values framework of the company, all on a day-to-day basis. You should target to get at least 30% of your employees to give free-text comments. Combined with quantitative data, qualitative input is a very powerful way of understanding patterns, addressing urgencies, and managing changes. At one company, we once experienced employees in key markets giving very low index scores for product offering and customer experience. At the same time, local free-text comments were full of the words like "out-of-touch," "complex," "slow," "Western aspiration," "Eastern affordability," and so forth. This combination became a real eye-opener for global leadership who launched a new way of localizing products and services as well as taking products and services to the local markets.

Free-text comments are useful at company and division level. For smaller units and teams, you would expect this improvement dialogue to happen orally in meetings, through regular feedback channels, and on a more frequent basis.

Employee photos of company values

Application: this metrics approach is most useful for organizations that are defining or renewing their company culture, values and behaviors, and/or ways of working and collaborating.

Description: photos made by employees contribute to making your company culture relevant and inspiring as well as enable the entire organization to live and breathe the desired values and related behaviors.

Calculation: a formula as such does not apply. A well-planned and well-executed project stipulating rules of participation, competitive terms, collection and evaluation of photos, and internal communications is evidently needed. Articulated commitment and active participation of leadership are needed, too.

Sample calculation: as an example, the leadership and communication teams have recently updated your three company values, "delighting customers," "being passionate about innovation," and "respecting the individual." To excite and involve all employees in bringing the values to life, you ask them to produce photos of the values. It is the intention to use the best photos as official images for each of the values in both internal and external communications.

Usage: participation in the competition should be representative of the full organization, office workers and factory workers, locations, etc. You may want to set targets for success at the outset. How many employees do you expect to participate as a threshold, percentage participation by location? How many photos must be delivered at a minimum? How many photos are targeted to pass the quality criteria? What topics do you expect to see in the pictures, and so on? Once the deadline for participation is past and all photos are in, what themes are occurring? What is surprising? What is this telling you about employee perceptions of company values? Are perceptions different by location or other demographic cut?

In a project in a company that I worked for, we saw an obsession with hands and feet as image themes, as well as most image themes coming from outside of work and showing employees' private lives. There were enough quality photos to justify project success, though one lesson learned certainly was to give more detailed guidance on theme framing: the corporate environment and work values.

Benchmarking and target setting

For all the metrics types outlined above—rate, ratio, composition, index, and qualitative input—benchmarks can be made available and targets for improvement set. Benchmarking is a relative comparison and provides meaning to an absolute standing. How do you know if this is a good or bad result? How do you know if this is a typical score? Relative comparisons indicate gaps and opportunities. Once you understand what gaps and opportunities exist, you use target setting to understand how to bridge gaps and realize opportunities.

With respect to benchmarking, there are external and internal norms and I will explore these a little further here.

External benchmarks

External benchmarks or norms for people data often focus on industry where you compare your results to an average industry benchmark. You may also want to raise the bar and compare to the top quartile or 75th percentile performing companies, regardless of industry, on the assumption that best practice is not industry-specific and there is a lot to learn from sustainably high-performing organizations.

Another alternative is to compare your organization with the "best companies to work for" in your country, geography, or globally. Fortune's Best Companies 2014 ranks Google as the number one employer in the U.S., based on a combination of the company's scores on a trust index, involving management's credibility, job satisfaction, and camaraderie, and a culture audit, including pay and benefit programs, hiring practices, methods of internal communication, training, recognition programs, and diversity efforts.[7]

The Reputation Institute, a reputation management consultancy which looks outside in, ranks companies on how well they meet consumer demands and are deemed trusted and relevant by consumers. The 2014 most reputable companies global ranking has Disney and Google in a shared number one position.[8] External benchmarks can be licensed for an annual fee from the relevant vendors. External benchmarks are aggregates by for example industry or geography, not company-specific.

Internal benchmarks

In contrast, internal benchmarks or norms are free-of-charge, specific for your company, and only your imagination will limit application and adaptation. Company overall averages and company cuts like region, country, function, and manager/not manager averages are obvious internal benchmarks. You can use top and bottom quartile benchmarks that will indicate leading and lagging segments and individuals. You can apply historical data where you compare one period to the previous one or two periods. Trend can also form an internal benchmark with improvements and declines in people data signaling leading and lagging segments and individuals.

You may want to study what highly scoring leaders and teams do and how they do it as well as document this internal best practice for other leaders and teams to learn from. There is often a wide distribution of scores in a company with long tail and extreme top scores. Articulating, understanding, and reproducing internal best practice is a characteristic of a high performance culture. Internal best practice signals that this happens in practice and is achievable, not only aspirational, in this company and workplace.

While benchmarking helps you make sense of your people data, target setting guides your change interventions and improvement actions across the business. A simple guide to target setting is to set aspirational, yet attainable objectives: aspirational objectives because you would not settle for second best and attainable objectives because you should feel you have a fair chance of success.

Smart targets

When setting targets, do it SMART. There are numerous definitions of smart target setting. In this context, SMART stands for Specific, Measurable, Achievable, Realistic, and Time-bound.

A **specific** target will usually answer the five "W" questions: What do we want to accomplish? Why is this important (reasons and benefits)? Who is involved? Where does this apply (location, function, group of people)? Which requirements and constraints do we foresee?

For a target to be **measurable**, it has a numerical value, an absolute number, a threshold for success, or an indicator for success.

Whether a target is **achievable** is for the key stakeholders, for example chair of steering group or project manager, to decide.

A **realistic** target states what results can realistically be achieved, given available resources.

A **time-bound** target indicates by when deliverables and results are expected.

The opposite of a SMART target is a DUMB (Dull, Unclear, Mundane, Boring) target. When you set targets, you may want to have some fun and first think up DUMB targets. How would this target be dull, unclear, mundane and boring for us to work with? Then turn negatives into positives. This is a kind of reverse brainstorming for target setting, which may result in more creative and stretching SMART targets and generate full commitment to fulfillment of the targets. In Table 3.3, you will find examples of SMART versus DUMB target setting for two improvement areas.

Table 3.3   Examples of SMART (Specific, Measurable, Achievable, Realistic, and Time-bound) versus DUMB (Dull, Unclear, Mundane, and Boring) targets

Target Area	SMART Targets	DUMB Targets
1. Reduction in high performers leaving the company	(S): Keep critical high performers/top talent as they contribute 3× average. Managers are responsible. Whole company. Possible need to raise reward. (M): Less than 7.5% high performer turnover rate. (A): Leadership team and HR deem achievable. (R): Industry benchmark is 10% and we want to be better. (T): Within 6 months.	(D): Trying to keep high performers, as this is what everybody does. (U): We cannot burden managers with this. (M): HR will make a plan. (B): The high performer turnover rate will gradually decrease over time if we just pay enough.
2. Increase in managers' participation in internal blogging	(S) Essential for strategy sharing and managers developing critical communications skills. A blog writing training is available. (M) More than 25% of managers active. (A) Head of Communications believes this is achievable. (R) 10% of managers are active today, training is available, and role modeling is encouraged. (T) Within 3 months, aligned with strategy dissemination process.	(D): The leadership team delegates this to managers. (U): There is no way we can ever achieve that! (M): Blogging is the new fancy thing; it does not apply in our business setting. (B): It has nothing to do with strategy.

Depending on current circumstances and expectations for the future, targets can be absolute or relative. Absolute targets remain fixed until the organization decides to change them. An example of an absolute target is for the company to set the target for their employee engagement index at 75% favorable. Relative targets change quarterly or annually, as benchmarks are updated and recalculated. An example of a relative target is for the company to specify that its employee engagement index must be between the 75th and 90th percentiles of the benchmark group.

Interpretation as foundation for driving change

Interpreting a human capital metric and the meaning of results provides the foundation for effectively and efficiently acting on people data and driving change. As exemplified in the outline of different metric types in this chapter, there are three useful steps in interpreting people data: translate metrics, contextualize results, and identify relevance.

Step one is about translating the metric. What is measured by the metric and what do the metric results tell me on a general level? What does an absolute result of XX% indicate?

Step two involves contextualizing results. What do metric results mean when read in the current business context? What do high results versus low results reveal? How do we compare to benchmarks? To what extent do results reflect our expectations and/or targets? What factors are surprising?

Step three is to identify relevance. Why is this particular people measurement topic important? How does it help us achieve our business goals? What impact does this measure have on human capital management? What can we do to build upon and improve scores? Where should your priorities be? How do we keep developing our strengths? How do we use feedback to improve and innovate around the way we work, collaborate, and compete?

In later chapters, we will dive into the process of understanding—sharing—acting on human capital metric and results and flesh out how to move from data to action.

Interplay of quantitative and qualitative data

Quantitative data is just numbers and formulas. During your interpretation efforts, there may be things you do not understand and want to investigate further. As mentioned, qualitative inputs, for example, free-text comments captured in surveys or on your intranet, can greatly enlighten you.

There are many ways of bringing data to life. Manager-to-manager conversations around people data, manager and team dialogues, and HR facilitation of focus groups are means to this end. When conversations, dialogues, and focus group findings are documented, these qualitative data sources can be analyzed alongside quantitative data sources.

A popular way of depicting text data is a word cloud that visually represents the most prominent single words and their importance by font size and color. For more thorough analysis, software tools for verbatim inputs exist. As a word of caution, you will need a good deal of data for this investment to pay off.

Another way of exploiting people data is using high or low scores to identify leading and lagging segments and individuals and further analyses and document what is going on in terms of best practice and worst practice. When the dos and don'ts are shared within the company, this becomes organization learning and agility as outlined earlier.

The organization's approach to sharing human capital metrics

Human capital metrics often sit in a variety of databases and tools and are not always freely accessible to the organization as a whole. The biggest part of using and applying human capital metrics in your company is that people data is available for all relevant audiences.

The spirit in which you use and apply people data will play an important role in how you approach availability and sharing. If you use and apply people data with the purpose of development in sight, it will be straightforward to freely and openly distribute the information. Development is to be understood broadly and includes the business, the organization, leadership, and talent. The purpose of using and applying people data is to develop, improve, and change quicker than competition. Many organizations use and apply people data with the purpose of assessing, supervising, and punishing. This is the opposite of the development and change approach and, in my opinion, does not create a win-win environment. The development spirit is forward looking, not backward looking. In Winston Churchill's words, "success is the ability to go from one failure to another with no loss of enthusiasm." The focus of broad development is longer term, doing what it takes, again and again, aiming for sustainable growth, not short-term optimization.

success is the ability to go from one failure to another with no loss of enthusiasm

It is interesting how hard it is for organizations to be or become fully transparent, especially in the current digital era. I have witnessed famous brand companies not wanting to share human capital findings freely on group level but where, ironically, subsidiaries or country organizations have published all data locally. Employees are not stupid and will get to the information anyhow. Less transparency stimulates speculations and rumors and ultimately creates a political climate where focus is distorted from the business. Full transparency supports focus, trust, and simplicity.

4

Determining What Measures You Need

Measuring the employee life cycle

There are a number of ways to go about identifying and prioritizing human capital metrics for your company. In Chapter 3, we looked at ten examples of different metric types:

1. Turnover rate
2. New hire % of high performers
3. Career Path Ratio
4. Operating profit per employee
5. Termination reason breakdown
6. Tenure distribution
7. Employee engagement index
8. Top talent recommendation
9. Free-text comments in survey
10. Employee photos of company values

These ten measures were selected because they are good illustrations of the different types of metrics we have: rate, ratio, composition, index and qualitative input. In addition, these metrics can be nicely plotted onto the talent management process to cover, to a greater or lesser extent, the span of talent decisions you as an organization leader are involved with throughout the employee life cycle. This relationship is shown in Table 4.1.

Table 4.1   Using the Employee Life Cycle to determine what metrics you need. The ten metric examples are from Chapter 3

Metric examples from Chapter 3	2	3, 4, 6, 7, 8, 9, 10	1, 5
Employee Life Cycle	Recruiting and on-boarding talent	Engaging, developing, leading, managing, and rewarding talent	Exiting talent

One way of determining what human capital metrics you need is that they would cover the spectrum of talent management objectives in your business. As illustrated in Table 4.1, the Employee Life Cycle is a good approach to ensure that all relevant talent decisions are covered by the metrics you prioritize for your company.

The remaining topics—or building blocks—covered in this chapter further help to frame what people data you need:

- Strategic choice and people fit
- Applying supply-chain thinking
- Johari Window to look beyond what is immediately visible
- People processes with the biggest bottom-line impact
- Global employee engagement drivers
- The concepts of people analytics and big data.

The first building block is your business strategy. Another building block is approaching talent management from a supply-chain angle where metrics help secure the pipeline and alleviate bottlenecks. And why not think broadly and boldly in order to avoid settling for what is easy to measure at the expense of what you really need to measure. It is also relevant to focus on the people processes with biggest bottom-line impact on your business, so called high Return On Investment (ROI) people processes. Yet another source of inspiration is the global factors driving employee engagement and characteristics of high performance organizations. Finally, there is the issue of how far you wish to take your measurement approach, with human capital metrics at one end of the scale, over people analytics, to big data at the other end of the scale.

Strategic choice and people fit

In the book *The Workforce Scorecard*, Huselid, Becker, and Beatty
outline the interdependence of strategic choice and people fit.[1] Even
though the importance of linking human capital metrics to your business strategy has already been underlined in Chapter 2, this point really
cannot be overemphasized. Aligning your people strategy with the
larger corporate strategy is a way of differentiating your workforce and
enabling targeted and calculated people decisions. If, like Wal-Mart,
your publicly stated strategic choice is cost leadership, your people fit
will be centered on process, stability, waste and costs avoidance, teamwork, and clear roles and responsibilities. If, like, Microsoft, your publicly stated strategic choice is product leadership, your people fit is more
about learning, challenging the status quo, discovery, cross-functional
collaboration, and leveraging ambiguity. Only when you are able to
identify those workforce capabilities, behaviors, and competencies that
genuinely give your company a competitive advantage will your people
become true assets to you. This is your X-factor!

With the strategy as starting point, I consider people
in the context of your company's full value chain.
People are a core driver of most strategies but
must work in concert with customers, suppliers,
and other stakeholders to create value. When linked
to your strategy, human capital metrics will speed-up and remove
execution obstacles, such as lacking customer focus, bureaucratic
behaviors dampening innovation capability, lacking competencies,
development needs, change resistance, people sitting on the fence, and
free-riding.

People are a core driver of most strategies

It is, of course, a huge motivational factor for people to see how they
fit into the big picture and how they contribute to the profit and
growth objectives of the business. So be passionate about sharing the
strategy in every corner of your business and articulate how people fit,
drive, and execute. I have plenty of evidence from surveying employees
in global companies that teams who have favorable perceptions of the
company's strategy sharing process also have higher engagement levels.

With a strategic perspective, you improve visibility to the people risks for your company. What talent is most important to the organization? What talent is most pivotal?[2] Pivotal talent exists where improving the quantity and quality of the talent has the greatest impact on organization success. And this is not always obvious. At Disney theme parks, for example, Mickey Mouse is important but not necessarily pivotal. The Mickey Mouse job is so well engineered that there is little payoff in improving the performance, once a high standard is met. In fact, Disney found the role of the park sweeper to be pivotal because guests often turn to sweepers with problems and questions. So, park sweepers are now looked upon as front-line customer representatives with brooms in their hands, trained to serve and support park visitors, and critical for customer loyalty. In your organization, what are the roles that would make or break the business? These are the roles to develop for improved performance and to guard against unnecessary turnover.

Grounding people measurement and management in the corporate strategy is also likely to be a good way of gaining commitment from your senior leaders that they and the managers they oversee will hold themselves accountable for the results and for improvements. When something is on senior management's agenda, it usually is on all organization leaders' agenda.

Applying supply-chain thinking

If we concentrate for a moment on the recruiting and on-boarding part of talent management as illustrated at the beginning of this chapter, I will now introduce you to how supply-chain thinking can be applied to determine what metrics are needed.

In the top row of the figure, the supply chain represents your talent pipeline (Figure 4.1). Individuals flow through the different filtering stages with the pipeline becoming smaller and smaller until you have identified the successful candidates and, eventually, your productive new hires.

Supply Chain: Talent Pipeline					
Talent pool → Applicant pool → Candidates → Offer candidates → New hires → Productive employees					
Planning	Recruiting	Screening	Selecting	Offering	On-Boarding
People Process: Recruiting and on-Boarding					

FIGURE 4.1 Applying supply-chain thinking to detailing people decisions and metric requirements

The recruiting and on-boarding process in the bottom row shows the activities and decision points, from planning talent demand and supply to on-boarding talent and removing barriers to performance.

The target is to define human capital metrics that will enhance your people decisions. Impactful recruiting and on boarding require measurement which will diagnose the quality of decisions of managers and applicants. Recruitment sources may be selected solely based on cost and volume of applicants. Recruiters may be selected solely based on availability (as well as all too often on personal relationship or subjective recommendation) and evaluated only on the volume of applicants they come up with. Applying supply-chain thinking helps measuring and managing the whole process, not merely isolated parts or activities such as planning, recruiting, screening, and so forth. Where are recruiting and on-boarding metrics sufficient? Where are they lacking, and where are they completely missing?

If we now dive deeper and focus on the "offering" part of the recruiting and on-boarding process, we can start to look for relevant measures for quality decisions. A couple of human capital metrics can be interesting. One is "offer acceptance rate." It is calculated as accepted offers in percentage of extended offers. This is especially useful, if you are sourcing talent from a highly competitive market, as it will indicate the effectiveness of the recruiting process, value of your employer brand, and strength of your offer to applicants, including such decision parameters as development opportunities and work environment on top of pay and benefits. High results on this metric (you want to be in the top 25% of an agreed upon benchmark group) mean high accuracy in the recruiting process and the offer. Low results may indicate issues with parts of the recruitment process, unacceptable perceptions of employer brand, managers' over- or underselling, or the offer being inadequate relative to competition.

Another interesting human capital metric for the offering process may be "rehire rate."[3] It is calculated as rehires in percentage of total external hires. For many companies, there will be productivity and cost advantages by hiring former employees and winning back the regretted losses you have suffered in the past. Rehires will need less on-boarding time and effort; they will know the company culture and processes, and be able to perform faster at full speed. Having or setting-up an alumni network supports rehiring of talent. You may want to aim to have 10% of new hires sourced from former employees, as this will secure you a nice stable supply to satisfy part of your overall talent demand.

In my experience, offer acceptance rate and rehire rate are a good cocktail to improve the quality of decisions of managers (and applicants) by bringing visibility and focus as well as balancing employer and employee objectives.

Johari window

Human capital metrics measure relationships in organizations: relationships aligning employees to the mission, vision, and strategy of the company, relationships enabling employees to develop and perform, relationships within teams, within departments, within divisions, and relationships between managers and employees. Human capital metrics are feedback to you as an individual performer, as an organization leader, and as groups of individuals. In determining what human capital metrics to work with, it is generally useful to think broadly and boldly.

The Johari Window, developed by two American psychologists, Luft and Ingham, in 1955,[4] is a concept for looking beyond what is immediately visible to others and to us. The Johari Window may help expand measurement and management of traits and aspects outside the organizational and individual comfort zones and encourage discovery of hidden and perhaps unique measures.

The first quadrant is open for all (Figure 4.2). The second quadrant represents behaviors and motives that are known to oneself, but not to others. The third "blind self" quadrant includes behaviors that are known to others, but not to oneself. The fourth "unknown" quadrant represents behaviors that no one recognizes. Human potential is unknown to us, and others; yet human potential is something we want to measure and manage in the corporate setting as part of performance management and talent calibration.

Assume for a moment that your strategic choice is product leadership. How do you determine human capital metrics to distinguish your people fit? You would probably want leaders who are good at coaching for performance and not micro-managing, who respect mastery, and who are obsessed with quality. Similarly, employees must be creative, good at dealing with ambiguity, passionate about the consumer experience, and enjoying a project-based way of working. It is very likely that some of

1	2
Known to self and organization	**Hidden from self and organization**
Things we know about ourselves and others know about us	Things we know about ourselves that others do not know
3	**4**
Blind to self and known to organization	**Unknown to self and organization**
Things others know about us that we do not know	Things neither we nor others know about us

FIGURE 4.2 / Using the Johari Window to identify metrics that will illuminate hidden characteristics, blind spots and unknown potential

your leaders have been experts themselves before becoming managers and might have a natural tendency towards micro-management. These managers are stuck in box 3, blind to this tendency that is known to the organization. Perhaps a creative employee cannot innovate on his or her own and needs a team round him or her to bounce ideas off. This is something he or she may be embarrassed or shy about and they hide this tendency from the organization, being stuck in box 2. Perhaps the obsession with quality is organization potential not recognized by leaders nor experts. This is unknown to self and to the organization. Well, proper human capital metrics would illuminate behaviors and relationships as well as support dialogues and decisions on people fit. Leaders' blind spots would be revealed in a manager quality index. A measure of living company values would enable employees to disclose their preferred ways of being creative and collaborating. Finally, quality obsession could be identified and leveraged if it was articulated as part of the company's high performance culture and measured by a high performance index.

In determining what human capital metrics to deploy, the first quadrant "know to self and organization" is probably representing what is most easy to measure, though not necessarily what you need to measure. In my experience with human capital metrics, laziness does not pay off, so settling for what is most obvious cannot be recommended. It is a good approach to broaden your perspective, not take too narrow a focus, and search beneath the surface of the obvious and known. Similarly, picking human capital metrics should not be limited by the availability of or ease of access to data. The Johari Window can be a reminder, too, of challenging constraints and seeking out alternatives. It is not the greatest of ideas to keep looking for the lost keys under the street lamp when you know you lost them in the dark alley.

Bottom-line impact of people processes

According to research from Boston Consulting Group, it pays off to be a people-oriented company with state-of-the-art people processes. "People" companies outperform the market average in terms of financial performance in eight out of ten years during the period from 2002 to 2011.[5] The people processes that have the biggest impact on your business' bottom-line include:

- Delivering on recruiting
- On boarding of new hires and retention
- Managing talent
- Improving employer branding
- Performance management and rewards
- Developing leadership

For these processes, the correlation between capability and financial performance is characterized as "impressive"; for example, companies adept at recruiting had 3.5 times the revenue growth and 2.0 times the profit margin of their less capable peers.[6] Furthermore, people companies are good at integrating critical people activities into their normal business processes and doing these activities in parallel and with all relevant stakeholder groups.

This is an inspiring pointer to where to focus your human capital measurement: the high-ROI people processes. Mastery of people management translates into financial success immediately. Determining what human capital metrics to use for managing bottom-line impact people processes may be key to creating human AND capital advantages!

Global drivers of employee engagement

Another approach for determining what metrics to aim for is to be inspired by what employees have for decades been telling organizations they really want from work. Putting a measurement framework around giving employees what they really want sounds quite intriguing actually and like a win-win approach.

In my various roles in overlooking employee engagement at global companies, I have been fortunate to have access to millions of data points. One of the most interesting findings is the fact that the key drivers of employee engagement are relatively consistent across geographies and stable over time. A key driver is usually established with statistical correlation analysis and can be verified by other statistical methods such as step-wise regression and discriminant analysis. In other words, the engagement key drivers can be validated to both influence and predict the outcomes companies target: discretionary effort (that extraordinary performance) and commitment (talent staying with the organization). On a global level, the top three most common employee engagement drivers I have come across are:

1. Confidence in senior leadership and future of the organization
2. Involvement and development
3. Culture on purpose with focus on diversity and work/life balance

The driver themes and survey results identified as most likely to influence engagement have been presented to thousands of divisions and teams based on the logic that action taken on any one of these priorities will drive positive change in engagement for the organization and the team. Action plans have been made, but real change seems difficult. Apparently, employees are not getting what they want from work and keep asking for the same things year after year, in countries and regions, consistently across the globe. Professional research institutions, for example, the Kenexa High Performance Institute,[7] echo the top driver themes for engagement that I have worked with. In the animate, the surprising truth about what motivates us,[8] Daniel Pink, career analyst, talks about purpose, mastery, and autonomy—three words that neatly summarize the global employee engagement drivers outlined above.

It is not too difficult to determine the human capital metrics that will establish and support the factors employees keep asking for. Table 4.2 provides a summary of improvement actions and metrics for the three key employee engagement drivers. This is a real-life example from a division I worked with in the past.

Determining the actions and metrics is not the difficult part, the difficulty lies in being persistent with your change efforts, involving all relevant stakeholders, monitoring progress on all levels of the divisions, and changing behaviors at the individual level (Table 4.2). In the example above, over a period of one year, engagement did, in fact, improve

Table 4.2   Actions and metrics/targets to satisfy employee engagement drivers

1. **Engagement driver**: purpose, confidence in vision and leadership
   a. **Improvement actions**: discussion in the leadership team on what our division part of the strategy is, how we fit in. Work by appointed group on new division strategy agenda.
   b. **Human capital metrics**: % favorable score for employee engagement index to increase.

2. **Engagement driver**: mastery, involvement, and development
   a. **Improvement actions**: listing and distinguishing division competences on a heat map, what competences are considered core, competitive, and differentiating. Discussion and documentation in Personal Development Plans (PDPs) on individual competencies and development needs.
   b. **Human capital metrics**: total cost of workforce flat. Build, not buy the best talent. Double training hours per employee.

3. **Engagement driver**: culture of autonomy, diversity, work/life balance
   a. **Improvement actions**: intranet blogs by leaders and employees. Monthly item on team meeting agenda.
   b. **Human capital metrics**: program/project steering groups > 5 nationalities. XX% of women in project manager roles. Stress level +/– 2% point compared to external benchmark.

significantly, though the drivers of engagement remained unchanged. This meant that while the improvement actions were updated and fine-tuned, the engagement drivers and human capital metrics continued to be valid and in use for several years.

What motivates us is existential, seemingly fairly stable, and hence a good basis for measuring and managing human capital in a globalized business world.

People analytics and big data

You will recall that in Chapter 1 we defined "human capital metrics" as quantitative and qualitative data points that companies collect to measure and manage people processes in the same way as financial metrics are collected to guide decision-making, performance, and compliance. Generally, human capital metrics are no different from people analytics and big data. All three constructs rely on data and that the data collected and reported are:

- Related to business needs
- Reliable and open to scrutiny
- Accompanied by adequate explanation
- Presented in an easily understandable manner
- Enabling organization leaders to identify appropriate actions that will improve business performance.

The difference lies in volume, sophistication of approach, and application.

People analytics is a data-crunching approach to managing people at work. People analytics models people-related processes ranging from recruitment through performance evaluation to promotion, their decision flows and decision weights, and then uses sophisticated data analysis for arriving at results. Perhaps it is fair to say that people analytics is using human capital metrics in a systematic way and attempts to bring very systematic processes to people decisions. Bigger companies mostly practice people analytics. One interesting story is from within the recruitment area where Xerox found that job candidates having a lot of experience working for different call centers is not necessarily a good thing. In fact, it indicated that job applicants had a high burnout rate and was a predictor of potentially bad performance. This is interesting because it is counterintuitive. Counterintuitive discoveries may not necessarily require people analytics, however, it probably requires a systematic, data-driven, and analytical approach.

Another story from within the recruitment arena is about robot recruiters and how software helps firms hire workers more efficiently.[9] Advocates of big data claim that dedicated software crunching piles of data will spot things not apparent to the naked eye. One such surprising correlation found by trailing millions of data points is that job applicants filling in online applications using browsers that did not come with the computer (such as Microsoft's Internet Explorer on a Windows PC) but had to be deliberately installed (like Firefox or

Google's Chrome) may be taking the right amount of time to reach informed decisions and should be better employees.

A few years ago almost no one had heard of "big data." Today it is hard to avoid. Big data refers to the idea that companies can do things with a large body of data that are not possible when working with smaller amounts. The term was originally applied a decade ago to massive datasets from astrophysics, voice-recognition machine learning, and Internet search engines. Now big data refers to the application of data analysis and statistics in new areas from retailing to human resources.[10] There are already some criticisms against big data like the biases inherent to data and the risks of spurious correlations (statistically robust but happening by chance) increasing with more data.

Answering the (billion-dollar) question of what people analytics will be able to do in five years from now that it cannot do today, Cade Massey, professor of information management at Wharton, believes it has to come from the big data side of things and the world of sports which is today the frontier of people analytics. The future of people analytics also depends on enough computing power and enough PhDs.[11] When it comes to talent management, "baseball" metrics are literally years ahead of human capital metric practices. What I find especially fascinating about baseball metrics is the fact that they are real-time and proprietary, allowing players and managers to make just in time and unique talent decisions.

chapter 5

A Toolbox for Managers

At the risk of oversimplifying things, I will endeavor to come up with a proposal for a human capital metrics toolbox for managers in this chapter. A toolbox is handy because it encourages you to take action and helps you get started, hopefully avoiding you doing nothing. You think about the job at hand and which tool(s) to bring along to fix it. Without a toolbox, you work with no tools or apply random tools.

A toolbox is handy because it encourages you to take action

First of all, the metrics to be included cover the span of decisions you, as an organization leader, typically need to make from recruiting and on-boarding employees through developing and managing people to exiting employees. In other words, the employee life cycle is used as a basis. Next, the determining factors of Chapter 3 have been used to prioritize a minimum set of basic metrics that supports organization leaders with securing, managing, and motivating employees to achieve business goals. The metrics represent strategic, high-ROI, and highly engaging people processes and activities. Last, but not least, all measures in your toolbox should be actionable!

This basic set of human capital metrics will enable you, as an organization leader, to start building your people acumen. All circumstances considered, it could be the beginning of a journey towards a more analytical and evidence driven culture in your company. It may not be fully comprehensive, nor entirely unique to your company, however, it is simple and solid and, as such, a good foundation to build upon.

Investigating who is accountable for talent management

Before we open the metrics toolbox, let us briefly reflect on who is accountable for talent management in your company? Do not laugh now, we all are. Employees, organization leaders, senior management, and HR (Human Resources) all play their part.

Each individual in the company, depending on their current role or roles, is engaged with talent management. As employees, we give feedback to and receive feedback from colleagues and managers. We participate in performance discussions. We care for and take care of our own talent and career development. We take ownership for improvement actions for teams, organizations, and ourselves. Organization leaders receive data and reports and, as part of their leadership role, initiate sharing and discussion activities around human capital metrics, one-on-one with the individual colleague or for the whole team and division. As leaders, we identify priorities for action and monitor and update actions. We also reflect on our own leadership competencies and how we develop ourselves as inspiring and motivating leaders. Senior leaders hold leaders and managers accountable for talent management activities in businesses and units and, together with senior HR leaders, align talent measurement and management with corporate strategy. HR colleagues own and manage the people processes, and tools, being experts on different parts, supporting and challenging leaders and managers on how to improve talent management, and collecting and sharing internal and external best practice. These are some examples of the ways everyone in the company is preoccupied with talent management, whether for their own benefit or the company's.

The human capital metrics toolbox has been designed with organization leaders in mind as the target audience. However, everyone in the company should be curious about how talent is measured and how talent is managed. We constitute the human capital of our organization, relevant and reliable metrics on the matter should be in everyone's interest and development of an analytical culture a desirable outcome for all, too. It is rather futile if managers prescribe the medicine and no one takes it. In order for the medicine to work, employees in all roles must develop an understanding of and reflect on what they need to do to meet the talent management objectives. In fact, as an employee, you might want to choose metrics from the toolbox to facilitate your own career development at various stages.

Talent management questions to be answered

Suppose you are a manager and human capital is more important to your business than physical capital. A set of key human capital metrics enabling you to make better data-driven decisions around the capabilities, behaviors, and competencies of your workforce will provide answers for the following talent management questions:

- How do I recruit for more diversity?
- How do we on board new hires and turn them into productive employees?
- As a manager, do I function as a launching pad for talent or do I tend to hoard talent?
- Which jobs do I need superstars in?
- If I push my training budget, does that have an impact on revenue per employee?
- What is the level of employee engagement in my team? What drives engagement in my team?
- How am I perceived as a manager? How can I develop my leadership capability?
- If I pay people less, will they still be committed?
- How many high performers are leaving and what are the reasons?

- Is there a need to rehire high-performing employees who left your company?
- Do I have the right people in the right place to execute my strategy?

Answers to these questions will come from either a single metric or a combination of several metrics and serve to guide your talent decisions and actions. You need to navigate along the talent management spectrum to ensure that you balance your efforts and focus on the right things at the right time.

Once you start focusing on talent management questions and getting human capital metrics to answer them, you will probably experience that the basic set of toolbox metrics is insufficient. By then, however, you will be in a better position to identify exactly what extra metrics are needed and you will probably also want to apply the toolbox metrics in new unique ways, to develop your own unique metrics, and to interlink different metrics while exploring assumptions and segmenting results. At this point, it may be useful to revisit Chapter 4 on "Determining What Human Capital Metrics You Need" to get inspiration and, for example, explore blind spots and unknown human potential by means of the Johari Window.

Data sources

In Chapter 2 on "Working Strategically with People," some fundamental considerations around people data are discussed. Data is the prerequisite for working with human capital metrics and needs to be complete, accurate, reliable, compliant, available, and timely. Gaps in data quality or data availability will slow you down, limit your analytics scope and constrain your people decision-making capability.

It is assumed in the following that your Human Resource Information System (HRIS) will provide you with basic quality data such as headcounts, turnover, promotions, and trend lines. Depending on how comprehensive your HRIS solution is, you may or may not have recurring and ad hoc project data included. An example of a recurring project is the employee engagement survey, which most organizations typically run bi-annually or annually. An example of an ad hoc project would be an end-to-end analytical process exploring the impacts of organization downsizing.

It is possible to talk about a data value curve as illustrated in Figure 5.1:

By adding and linking different data, the organization builds analytical and evidence-based capacity around people decisions.

- The data value curve begins with reactive checks and ongoing reports being based on your HRIS and bespoke HR tools.
- More data value is added with benchmarks and insights coming from project data and ad hoc queries.
- Additional data value in the form of predictions will come from linkage of HR data sources and operational data on for example quality and profit.

HRIS is the data foundation. HRIS can hold data for all talent management activities or data from specific processes will sit in bespoke tools. If, for example, performance management data is outside HRIS in a separate software solution, data feeds will secure availability of human capital metrics from one integrated source. Project data is typically found in separate tools and needs to be integrated into HRIS (or a data warehouse solution) for further analysis. The same goes for operational data. Let us say you want to analyze if your highly engaged teams actually deliver the best quality or are, in fact, the most profitable.

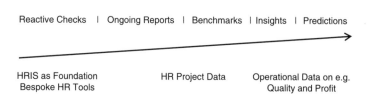

Reactive Checks | Ongoing Reports | Benchmarks | Insights | Predictions

HRIS as Foundation   HR Project Data   Operational Data on e.g.
Bespoke HR Tools   Quality and Profit

FIGURE 5.1 Data value curve and how different data builds evidence driven and analytical capacity in the organization

There are many factors affecting how advanced you aim to be on the data value curve. One of these variables will be the level of resources to be devoted to managing human capital.

Once we open the toolbox, it will be specified for each metric included how data is normally sourced.

Inside the toolbox

The toolbox covers the full talent management process and includes 11 different metrics. In numerology,[1] the number 11 is the first of the master numbers and usually called the illuminator, the messenger, or master teacher, so 11 measures it is! A toolbox filled with illuminations, messages, and teaching materials is not a bad aid for you to become more able to make appropriate people decisions and take sufficient actions in most of the situations you face. You get an overview of the different human capital metrics included in the toolbox from Table 5.1.

In the following, each of the 11 metrics will be detailed in terms of why this metric is important, what questions it helps to answer, and how it is typically sourced and used (Table 5.1). In contrast to Chapter 3, "The Machine Room," outlining the different types of metrics and providing broader and more general application and usage guidelines for each metric type, the focus here is on how you, as an organization leader, use and apply specific human capital metrics:

- Four of the metrics in the toolbox for managers are the same as in Chapter 3, but now the angle is the manager, not the whole company: new hire % of high performers (3), employee engagement metric (4), career path ratio (6), and termination reason breakdown (11).
- Rehire rate (2) was briefly touched upon earlier in Chapter 4, "Determining What Human Capital Metrics You Need."
- Otherwise the remaining metrics in the toolbox are new and will be introduced in the present chapter.[2]

Table 5.1   The eleven human capital metrics covering the Employee Life Cycle included in the toolbox

Metric Number	Recruiting and On Boarding Talent	Engaging, Developing, Leading, Managing, and Rewarding Talent	Exiting Talent
1. Diversity distribution	X		
2. Rehire rate	X		
3. New hire high performers % of high performers	X		
4. Employee engagement index		X	
5. Manager effectiveness index		X	
6. Career path ratio		X	
7. Training hours per full-time employee		X	
8. Job heat map		X	
9. Average annual salary per full-time employee		X	
10. Turnover rate high performers			X
11. Termination reason breakdown			X

The section "Why this metric is important" gives a general description of the measure and reasons for its relevance. The section "What questions the metric helps to answer" includes the metric formula, questions appropriate to this measure, what the metric does not cover and where further investigation may be needed. The section on "How the metric is sourced and used" provide input on data sources and how managers get hold of this people data, examples of how this measurement is applied, as well as guidance on targets and benchmarks, where applicable.

I believe that when leaders and managers ask relevant human capital questions and actively request people data, also in new forms, this has the potential to greatly enhance talent management capabilities and make decisions for the workforce across the business more data-driven and future-proof.

Diversity distribution

Why this metric is important

Putting diversity on the agenda is important for several reasons. Diversity measures often have to be reported externally to country authorities and in sustainability reporting as required by United Nations' Global Compact guideline.[3] Marketing advocates would claim that your organization should be as diverse as the marketplace in which you compete, so that all employees think and act like the customers they serve. A Diversity Distribution metric is also important because diverse teams, when well functioning, are more innovative. Everyone who has worked in a well-functioning diverse team recognizes the feeling of how 2 plus 2 may come to equal 5.

What questions the metric helps to answer

Diversity Distribution shows a breakdown into parts with numbers and/or percentages allocated to each part. "Diversity" is a broad term and you have to narrow it down to what aspects of diversity are essential to your company (and what kinds of diversity data your HRIS holds). The Diversity Distribution metric could include: age, gender, function (sales, marketing, design, finance, etc.), nationality, position (senior management, manager with subordinates, project manager, technical expert, administrative staff, factory workers, etc.) and tenure, with tenure often being a proxy for the employee's age or life stage. In Chapter 3, a formula for Tenure Distribution is provided:

End of period headcount by tenure type/end of period headcount × 100. And the sample calculation provided is: 50 employees with < 1 year tenure/500 total headcount × 100 = 10%.

This is the pattern for building the Diversity Distribution. If you have a spare moment (yes, I am serious), you could easily build your own bespoke Diversity Distribution. Or you could ask HR for a template, filled or unfilled.

Questions this metric helps to answer include:

- How does your Diversity Distribution reflect the marketplace in which you compete?
- Where are the gaps? Which gaps are biggest? Which gaps are most important?
- How do you compare to other similar teams in the organization?

What this metric does not cover and where further investigation may be needed:

- How do you fill the gaps in your Diversity Distribution?
- What would your team say about the degree of diversity, how satisfied are they with the current set-up, and what would they like to change?
- How does your current distribution map to your company's growth strategy?

How the metric is sourced and used

Data on diversity dimensions such as age, gender, function, nationality, position, and tenure are typically found in your HRIS database. If you cannot get this data from the company HRIS, you can collect it for yourself to build your Diversity Distribution.

The Diversity Distribution will point towards the DNA of your team. Your advantage is that you can change the DNA when you get the opportunity. For example, when an employee leaves, you can try to recruit for more diversity. The same goes for all the diversity dimensions you deem important. High levels of similarity may drag the organization in one particular direction whereas high levels of diversity will tend to balance things out and make it possible to hit on all cylinders. As a manager, you get exposed to a variety of personalities, expectations, and aspirations and such exposure will prepare you in the best way for future leadership challenges. You broaden your views and limit your prejudices.

Variations on core measures provide flexibility to focus on the areas of greatest interest to your team/division. In the case of diversity, you define the variations that are most useful in your scenario while maintaining simplicity.

Rehire rate

Why this metric is important

Rehire Rate is important, because talent is scare. Most companies will fight for, perhaps not all, but definitely part of their talent, and depending on industry and geography, this can be a big part. Being aware of the possibility to re-recruit former employees is a first step. Rehiring them is the next step. The regrettable turnover of the past is of special interest. In order to rehire people, it is essential that you as a manager manage the exit process of colleagues in a professional way. Your chances of rehiring them diminish with poor leadership capabilities. Rehires are assumed to become highly productive employees in a short time period.

Most companies will fight for, perhaps not all, but definitely part of their talent

What questions the metric helps to answer

Rehire Rate is calculated as rehires in percentage of total external hires. A sample calculation is: 3 rehires/15 all external hires × 100 = 20%.

Questions this metric helps to answer include:

- What is my capability as a networker?
- How is my standing within various communities (alumni, expert forum, etc.)?
- How is my organization's ability to keep connected with former high-performing colleagues?
- How attractive is my team to work with?
- What level of productivity exists?

What this metric does not cover and where further investigation may be needed:

- How long has the rehired employee been away from the organization?
- How long was the rehired employee employed by the organization before terminating and moving to another employer?
- Where rehiring is particularly important, e.g. in a certain geography, for a particular job function, or for a specific position.

How the metric is sourced and used

Rehire Rates typically come from your HRIS where rehires are flagged by different action codes than other hires. You may also keep a register of rehires and all external hires on your own initiative; this should not be too difficult.

You use the Rehire Rate to solve people demand-supply constraints as well as to balance costs and efforts in relation to recruiting, on boarding, and productivity. This is a chance to bring back good people you regretted losing in the past. Former employees will know how things are done here, from processes to culture, and may alleviate the induction and on-boarding tasks of managers and teams.

Having or setting-up an alumni network supports the rehiring of talent. Networking in relevant forums and communities by the manager and the team members also support relationship building and connections being kept alive. Encourage your team members to be good networkers by walking the talk as a manager! You may want to target to have 10% of new hires sourced from former employees (or more, if you demand is much bigger than supply). Following the Rehire Rate ensures a stable supply of experienced talent and satisfies a certain proportion of your overall talent demand.

New hire high performers % of high performers

Why this metric is important

New Hire High Performers % of High Performers is important because it demonstrates how impactful your recruiting and on boarding of new employees is. Leaders and managers play a key role in this part of the talent management process. You recruit and on board for high performance. New hires come in engaged and ready to be productive from day one—and there is only *one* day one—and it is the responsibility of the recruiting manager, together with HR, to ensure the work environment is welcoming and embracing so that talent can quickly and easily unfold.

What questions the metric helps to answer

New Hire High Performers % of High Performers is calculated as newly hired employees with high performance rating/all high performers × 100. A sample calculation is:

2 new hire high performers/8 all high performers × 100 = 25%.

You need to define what you mean by "new hire" in your company, is it employees who have been employed for 1, 3, 6, or 12 months. You also need to lean on your company's definition of "high performer." A common way of performance rating is to use a scale from 1 to 3 or 1 to 5, with the highest number indicating high performance.

Questions this metric helps to answer include:

- What is my capability as a recruiting manager?
- What is my organization's ability to attract high performers?
- How do I as a manager on board new hires, coach for performance, and turn new hires into productive employees?
- How do we as a team live and breathe a high performance culture?

What this metric does not cover and where further investigation may be needed:

- How robust is our performance rating, is the performance management process accommodating for all types of talent?
- How well is the performance management process understood by new hires? Has it been communicated in an engaging manner?
- What parts of the process that I can control need to be improved?
- What parts of the process outside my control need to be escalated for improvement?

How the metric is sourced and used

New Hire High Performers % of High Performers is sourced from your HRIS or a separate performance management tool in combination with your HRIS. Performance ratings typically take place on an annual basis so you will only get this metric once a year. Based on the template and approach used by the company, you may keep track of how your new hires are doing on a more regular basis, e.g. monthly, and discuss your observations with the new hires. This will also help new hires get familiar with the performance management process at your company and set them up for ongoing success. Keeping your own record is not difficult; you use the denominator (all high performers in your team/division) from the annual company calculation and decide on the numerator based on your own observations and feedback from colleagues and customers. The calculation can be done in your head for smaller teams and no software or calculator is needed.

You use New Hire High Performers % of High Performers metric to monitor how effectively the manager and the team on board new team members. New hires are recruited based on thorough testing for high performance in the selection process. However, all too often, high performers with an excellent past track record and recruiting test outcome may not be enabled to do their best work in the new work environment. Having spent a lot of time and money on recruiting the best talent, you may say your reputation is on the line. New talents ending up as poor performers are really not an option. If you target to have more than 15% of new hires in the high-performing segment, this would generally mean you are doing a good job of on boarding new employees. Most companies have limits for how many employees can be high performers and all colleagues compete to be in this limited space. New hires quickly becoming high performers may require high maintenance. They will put pressure on you to continue to fully utilize, develop, and coach them.

For this metric you may want to understand how you stack up against other managers in your company. HR would be able to provide such internal benchmarks from the central HRIS. There may be a company overall benchmark, a functional or country benchmark, and junior/senior manager benchmarks.

Employee engagement index

Why this metric is important

The employee engagement index will tell you how motivated your people are to contribute (discretionary effort) and stay (retention) as well as the level of pride they take in being part of achieving your company's vision. The Employee Engagement Index is what is called an outcome measure. No one can force you to go the extra mile. No one can tell you to be proud of working for your company. The index gives a level of engagement. In order to improve the engagement level, decisions and actions should be directed at all the factors influencing engagement, such as the work itself, work environment, the team, the manager, customers, and company culture. In the next chapter, I will take you through the end-to-end process of how to use and apply employee engagement in an organization.

What questions the metric helps to answer

The Employee Engagement Index is a relative measure of your employees' engagement with the organization. You can build the Employee Engagement Index according to your preference. It can consist of one or several statements which employees rate according to a predefined scale. I previously used the following calculation for demonstration purposes:

Average of % favorable scores of question statements in the index, that is (Q1 % favorable + Q2 % favorable + Q3 % favorable)/3.

Questions this metric helps to answer include:

- How engaged is my staff, assuming the Employee Engagement Index predicts discretionary effort and willingness to stay?
- How proud are my people to work in your company?
- To what extent would employees recommend your company as a great place to work?
- What drives engagement in my team? What makes us successful as a team? What holds us back?
- What are the things in my control that I can do to further improve engagement levels? What can we do together?
- What additional help do we need?

What this metric does not cover and where further investigation may be needed:

- How high engagement links to actual high performance, quality, or profit?
- What drives what? Does engagement drive business success or business success engagement?

- What is best practice in my company?
- What do best-in-class people companies do? Why do they get nominated "Best Company to Work For"?[4]

How the metric is sourced and used

Data for this metric is typically sourced from the responses to one or more question statements in employee surveys. Your central HR team will orchestrate the employee engagement process. Some companies like to take the pulse of the organization more frequently, for example on a quarterly basis, whereas others prefer to survey only every second year. In today's fast-paced work world and VUCA (volatility, uncertainty, complexity, ambiguity) times, I would say an annual survey is the minimum.

As a manager, you will get the survey results for your team/division, probably in an email as a document attachment or a link to an online tool. It is your responsibility to put the data to work in the team/division and facilitate the necessary changes. You would take a private moment to understand your results and then discuss results with your manager. You would want to have a discussion around division results within your leadership team. You would circulate results with the team in advance of a sharing and action-planning meeting. At the meeting, the team starts to identify strengths, weaknesses, what we already have with the present scores, what would be different with a higher score, and what the leadership, the manager, the colleagues, and the individual should do to change things for the better.

You would normally have a number of benchmarks at hand, both external like your industry norm and high-performing companies norm, and internal like company average, company Top 25%, and country/function benchmark. These benchmarks can be found in Chapter 6.

Manager effectiveness index

Why this metric is important

The relevance of the Manager Effectiveness Index is fairly self-evident. No one aspires to be an ineffective manager. The Manager Effectiveness Index will tell you how your employees perceive you as a manager. It will as such cover all the situations where you lead them from strategy sharing to team building to individual coaching. Effective leadership can be learned. By being aware of what good leadership is, as defined in your company and best practice, and being measured accordingly, you have the means to develop your leadership and management capabilities.

What questions the metric helps to answer

The Manager Effectiveness Index is a relative measure of your employees' perceptions of how you lead and manage them. The index will typically reflect the leadership model in use at your company and is coordinated by the central HR team. It consists of several statements that are rated by employees on a predefined response scale. Effective leadership and management are about competencies and behaviors such as treating employees respectfully, giving ongoing feedback to help performance improvement, encouraging employees' development at work, building a strong team, supporting execution of the strategy efficiently, and inspiring the best in people.

You may have noticed that the terms leadership and management are used alongside each other in this book and may wonder why this is the case and what the difference is between these terms. It is intentional to use leadership and management together. However, they are different constructs. According to John P. Kotter, Professor with Harvard Business School, the confusion around these two terms is massive, however, leadership and management must co-exist as they serve different functions.[5] Management is a set of well-known processes, like structuring jobs and measuring performance, which helps an organization to do what it knows how to do well. In contrast, leadership is about vision, the future, and people buying into it, empowerment, finding opportunities, and making necessary positive changes. Both leadership and management are required from organization leaders, no matter where they sit in the hierarchy. Quoting Kotter: "The notion that a few extraordinary people at the top can provide all the leadership needed today is ridiculous, and it's a recipe for failure."[6]

leadership and management must co-exist as they serve different functions

Hence, an impactful Manager Effectiveness Index will include both kinds of competencies and behaviors.

Questions this metric helps to answer include:

- How am I perceived as a leader and manager?
- What is surprising to me? What am I happy with and what am I unhappy about?
- How do I compare to external/internal benchmarks?
- What am I going to do about it?

What this metric does not cover and where further investigation may be needed:

- How can the team help me to develop?
- How can my manager and leadership team help me to develop?
- What training and development opportunities exist?
- Who can coach me? Where do I find more inspiration?

How the metric is sourced and used

Data for this metric is typically sourced from the responses to question statements in employee surveys or 360-degree feedback routines, which are run and facilitated by your central HR team.

You will get access to your results, as part of the employee engagement survey, or a dedicated feedback tool. Take some time to reflect on results. What surprises you? What worries you? You should ask your HR business partner to guide you through your results with a focus on a couple of key take-aways for you. What are the one or two key things you should do more of or less of? Together with your manager and HR, you explore what help is available, for example, leadership training, getting a coach, shadowing a leader or leadership team, or reverse mentoring where a younger employee would mentor you.

For this metric there should be external and internal benchmark available. A common approach is to rank managers according to their quartile position, meaning you would be in first, second, third or fourth quartile. This makes it easy to set improvement targets, move from one quartile to the next, or within the top quartile to a better position here. It is easier, too, to monitor progress.

The Manager Effectiveness Index is often used in performance evaluation of organization leaders, for the "how" part of the evaluation (the other part is the "what"). Another common way the Manager Effectiveness Index is applied is as one criterion in promotion decisions.

Career path ratio

Why this metric is important

The Career Path Ratio will help answer the talent management question posed above "As a manager, do I function as a launching pad for talent or do I tend to hoard talent." Most organizations are pyramid-shaped or hierarchical which means you have limited upwards mobility but almost unlimited sideways mobility. Try to look at the bigger picture when you discuss career opportunities with your people, also your best people. Work as a launch pad and send high performers sideways! They may come back to you later or you move upwards yourself and you can bring them with you at a later stage.

What questions the metric helps to answer

The Career Path Ratio measures total promotions relative to total transfers, with "promotion" being an upward movement in the organization and "transfer" being a lateral movement. The formula is: total promotions/total transfers. A sample calculation is: 2 promotions/6 transfers = 0.3. For every employee you promote, you transfer 3. It is relatively easy to keep track of your Career Path Ratio on your own initiative or with the help of your HR business partner.

Questions this metric helps to answer include:

- How do I coach people for performance?
- How many employees do I promote? How many do I transfer?
- Do I tend to hoard talent?
- What is the relationship between my promotions and my transfers?
- Do I tend to function as a launch pad?

What this metric does not cover and where further investigation may be needed:

- How many people join my organization?
- How do I hedge my losses?
- Is what I do is similar to other managers? How do we best support the business?
- When does being a good corporate citizen pay off? When does it not pay off?
- How well do the people I promote execute in their new roles?
- Do the people I transfer leave the company subsequently?

How the metric is sourced and used

Data on workforce career development and promotion is part of the HRIS. Career Path Ratio shows the degree of upwards movement versus lateral movement within your team or division. If your ratio is between 0.5 and 1, you are hoarding talent. There are more possibilities of moving sideways than upwards so you may want your ratio to be below 0.2 (depending on industry and company size). Career Path Ratio will indicate the extent to which you are a good corporate citizen. However, if other managers are not letting their people go, you will have a hard time finding new people internally. This may mean that you get punished by an increase in recruitment costs. As it is in the interest of the whole company that good people stay, there should be general company-wide agreement on Career Path Ratio levels. As mentioned earlier, all managers benefit from letting talent roam free inside the company; you give some and you get some.

Training hours per full-time employee

Why this metric is important

Managers' encouraging employees' learning and development at work is important. Training hours per employee is an indicator of the average number of training hours for each full-time employee. It helps you monitor your development plans and training budgets and allows you to benchmark individual team members against average consumption in your team (or whole company) or, if external data is available, industry or high-performing companies levels.

What questions the metric helps to answer

The formula is: total training hours/full-time employees. "Full-time employee" may be HR jargon, however, you will probably want to exclude part-time employees and focus on training volume for employees with full-time status. This metric is most often used for formal training only, which is more costly in terms of money but not in terms of time. The 70–20–10 training model commonly in use suggests that effective learning comprises of 70% on the job, 20% from managers and peers, and 10% from formal training like courses and reading.[7] It is worth noting that 21st century employees do not physically need (or want) to leave their working environment to carry out formal training.

Questions this metric helps to answer include:

- How do I as a manager get the most out of the formal training for my employees? How do I best leverage that investment for the company and for the individual?
- How do the formal training days complement on-the-job learning and feedback from managers, peers, and customers?
- How do I utilize the 70–20–10 training model?
- How do I keep my training budget in turbulent times?

What this metric does not cover and where further investigation may be needed:

- How effective is the formal training? What is the impact on revenue per employee?
- How do we increase learner usage of training programs?
- How do development benefits outweigh training costs?
- What could I do better? What should my involvement be? How do I compare internally or externally?
- What is thought leadership on formal and informal, social, workplace, experiential learning and development?

How the metric is sourced and used

Data for this metric would be sourced from a learning management tool or other database where training is recorded and tracked. You need to be quite meticulous with tracking each training occurrence and its duration.

A frequently used benchmark for this metric is 40 hours per year. If you invest heavily in developing your human capital, you may aim to be in the 75th percentile of a relevant benchmark group. Training hours depend on industry. Be cautious that the learning management tool only includes formal training or the 10% of learning and development model.

Another important measure comes from the Employee Engagement survey where employees rate the extent to which they feel they are developing in their role and on-the-job. You find more on the Employee Engagement process in Chapter 6 where questions on learning and development are included in the "work" theme of the survey questionnaire example.

Job heat map

Why this metric is important

A Job Heat Map is a way of segmenting the jobs within your team or division and pointing attention to those jobs that make a clear and positive difference in your ability to succeed in the marketplace. In Chapter 4, the concept of pivotal talent was exemplified with the sweeper role at Disney Theme Parks. Pivotal talent exists where improving the quantity and quality of the talent has the greatest impact on organization success.

What questions the metric helps to answer

A heat map is a composition type of metric where you break down your team or division into parts while allocating the level of significance or differentiation to each part. Below you find an illustration of such a heat map showing what processes/jobs are most significant and differentiating. This is a high level illustration and you would need to make the effort, with the help of your HR business partner, to produce the kind of heat map that applies to your reality.

This heat map identifies which processes/jobs are *core* (necessary to stay in business but not differentiating in the marketplace), *competitive* (potential customers consider you), and *differentiating* (customers' buying decisions are directed towards you) (Figure 5.2). Performance variation in the competitive and differentiating jobs is likely to be more valuable than in the core jobs.[8] A heat map may start an inspiring conversation about performance variation and what it means for your teams.

Questions this metric helps to answer include:

- What and where are my core, competitive, and differentiating roles?
- How do the existing people I have in the roles perform?
- What development is needed?
- Where do I focus my attention?
- What does this mean in terms of recruiting?

What this metric does not cover and where further investigation may be needed:

- What are the specific skills needed in each role?
- What are the expenses associated with each role?
- How do I reshuffle roles?
- What I am missing that I will need in the future?

Marketing and Sales	Product	Supply Chain	Business Administration
Brand strategy	Supplier strategy	Transportation planning	People strategy and planning
Campaign management	Product lifecycle management	Supplier performance management	HR processes
After sales services	Product allocation	Services delivery	HR payroll

Core	Competitive	Differentiating

FIGURE 5.2 Heat map showing organization processes and jobs that are most differentiating

How the metric is sourced and used

Job role specifics and functional assignments are part of your HRIS, however, you are likely not to find the level of granularity you need and you would, in any case, have to fill in the heat map by yourself with help from HR.

Identifying pivotal talent and differentiating roles means understanding where and how your division plans to compete and then target to improve performance in these areas. The Job Heat Map will support you in getting an overview of how your people fit within the core, competitive, and differentiating roles and identify gaps and risks. The employees in your differentiating jobs are probably also at risk for talent poaching and represent current and future labor market shortages.

Average annual salary per full-time employee

Why this metric is important

Average Annual Salary per Full-Time Employee is perhaps not the most exciting metric in the toolbox. However, as compensation for most organizations is a major, if not the largest, operating expense, it is an important measure. In addition, employees would perhaps consider base pay to be the most important part of your employment offer. In the global business context, your R&D engineers in India and the US or shared services employees in Germany, Poland, and Vietnam are on different salary levels though comparable to local benchmarks.

What questions the metric helps to answer

Average Annual Salary per Full-Time Employee shows the average base salary of a full-time equivalent employee, excluding bonuses and other non-wage compensation. It is calculated as total annual salary/full-time employees.

Questions this metric helps to answer include:

- How do the average salary levels in my function compare country by country?

- How do I compare to internal and external benchmarks? How do I trend year-on-year? How do I manage this expense?
- What kind of adjustments should I make, up or down?
- How do I compensate different talents relative to the average for my function?
- Where do I want/need to perform this work, and at what cost?

What this metric does not cover and where further investigation may be needed:

- What kind of salary variations exist relative to diversity differences? For example, am I paying women less than men?
- How satisfied are employees with the salaries?
- How do I comply with company policy, country by country?

How the metric is sourced and used

Annual salary data and headcount are sourced from your HRIS. Alternatively, salary payments may be sourced from the payroll system.

You use the Average Annual Salary per Employee to manage your salary costs, which most probably constitute a major expense. You benchmark for compliance with company pay philosophy and employee expectation. You make adjustments and differentiations according to your findings. To answer the question asked earlier "If I pay people less, will they still be committed," you compare your employee engagement index and salary levels over time to check how they correlate. You may experiment with compensating extrinsic motivation factors (coming from outside the individual like pay and non-monetary recognition) with intrinsic motivation factors (coming from inside the individual like achievement of a challenging task and passion for what we do in this team). This experiment will indicate if less monetary reward is possible while maintaining or even improving commitment and sustaining performance.

Turnover rate high performers

Why this metric is important

In Chapter 3, the overall turnover rate is illustrated. For you as a manager, perhaps the turnover rate of your high performers is more interesting.

In either case, the concept is the same and you can choose to work with the one metric that you find most suitable for your situation. Or you can work with both and utilize the comparison between the two. As stated in Chapter 3, if your overall turnover rate is lower than your Turnover Rate High Performers, depending on the size of the gap, you may be bleeding talent. Turnover Rate High Performers, also in combination with the Termination Reason Breakdown to follow below, is a powerful way of monitoring if the deal you offer talent is competitive and how you manage to retain high-performing staff currently and over time.

What questions the metric helps to answer

The formula for Turnover Rate High Performers is the total number of high-performing employees that terminated in a given period/the average high performer population in your team/division over the same period × 100.

Questions this metric helps to answer include:

- How many high-performing employees are leaving my team/division?
- Combined with the Termination Reason Breakdown, what can I do to stop it?
- How do I replace my regrettable turnover?
- How do I ensure proper knowledge transfer and handover from high-performing employees?

What this metric does not cover and where further investigation may be needed:

- What can my company do to retain high performers?
- Where are the high performers going?
- What do competitors do?
- What are the cost implications, if any?

How the metric is sourced and used

The termination data is typically sourced from your HRIS. High performance ratings are sourced from the performance management part of your HRIS or within separate performance management systems.

The level of high performers leaving you will indicate something about what you are offering, both in terms of extrinsic drivers such as rewards and benefits, but probably more in terms of intrinsic drivers. Is your team a hot spot to be? What kinds of development and career opportunities are available? Is the job making good use of ambitious people's knowledge, skills, and abilities? Do you adapt quickly to changing customer demands? Are you as a manager inspiring the best in people?

Again, for this metric you may want to understand how you stack up against other managers in your company. HR would be able to provide such internal benchmarks from the performance management system.

Termination reason breakdown

Why this metric is important

As mentioned earlier, most companies fight for talent. You need to understand and be able to act on why people leave, especially the high-performing talent that you have cared and catered for during their employment. Getting an overview of the numerous reasons for employee departures will no doubt also take some of the burden off your shoulders as a manager—if you are a fair manager, you are seldom the reason behind regrettable turnover.

What questions the metric helps to answer

The Termination Reason Breakdown provides a distribution of terminations during a reporting period by type and reason for termination. Termination types are typically involuntary, voluntary, and high-performing leavers. To recap, involuntary leavers are people who you let go and voluntary leavers are people who leave of their own initiative. You need to define the termination reasons that apply to your company. In Chapter 3, a sample calculation is provided, from where you can see some typical reasons. The metrics are calculated like this: termination-by-termination reason/all terminations × 100.

You may want to see absolute numbers as well as percentages in the distribution.

Questions this metric helps to answer include:

- Why are people leaving my team/division? What are the patterns, if any?
- What are the different reasons for voluntary and high-performing leavers?
- Whether we have let high-performing staff go as part of re-structuring initiatives?
- What can I immediately do to stop high performers from exiting?

What this metric does not cover and where further investigation may be needed:

- How do we improve as a company?
- What effects does this have on my team? Can I expect more resignations?
- What are leavers not telling us?
- How do employees who stay feel?

How the metric is sourced and used

Terminations are sourced from the HRIS where they would typically be mapped to the type of termination and the reason. Another more granular data source is an exit survey which is sent out to all leavers and where the leaver's performance rating and termination type is brought over from the HRIS. Reporting would not happen on individual employee level but be aggregated on a minimum number of individuals to safeguard confidentiality.

You should explore the reasons why people are leaving your team/division carefully. Is there a pattern and, if so, how can it be broken quickly. You should sort out what can you do that is under your control and what needs to be escalated. Voluntary terminations due to manager relationship are a particular area for scrutiny. Reflect back on your relationship with this employee, what could you have done differently, and how do you take this learning forward.

What is in it for managers?

Before we close the toolbox chapter, it may be an idea to recap what is in it for me as a manager:

- Being equipped with a toolbox is a good start. It is a beginner's toolbox. You have 11 tools available. Like a hammer is used for a specific purpose, so is each of the 11 metrics meant to serve a specific talent management scenario. The New Hire High Performers % of High Performers is used to manage on boarding of new employees and the Job Heat Map to segment, lead, and develop people for core, competitive, and differentiating jobs.
- You can play around with the tools in the toolbox. In some situations, you need a hammer and a drill. You mix and match metrics according to purpose. The Turnover Rate High Performers tells you that you have been losing too many high performers lately. You use the Termination Reason Breakdown in combination with the Turnover Rate High Performers to investigate the reasons why and to take appropriate action to stop high performers from exiting.
- Looking at all these measures once is not enough! It is just a snapshot. Looking at trends and benchmarks adds much more value.
- You are gradually displaying more and more people acumen. You become keen on understanding and dealing with people situations and quick in solving matters with good outcomes.
- You know you do not have all the answers! You ask more questions, do not only rely on what worked in the past, but stay open-minded and humble, and reflect on ramifications, before you make your people decisions. You become a leader who people want to follow. Your brand value as a manager of people is increasing.
- You experience the ripple effect. With the metric Average Annual Salary per Full-Time Employee, you keep costs under control. On top of financial benefits, there are non-financial effects of reputation and citizenship. You are part of building the employer brand of your company as a place where people are being treated respectfully and fairly.
- You are among the first movers and early adapters on the journey towards a more analytical culture in your company.

Making It Happen

How to apply people data

Once you have your measurement approach, your toolbox implemented and begun working with your metrics, the next challenge is applying the metrics and turning your data into action. In fact, the most damaging (and costly) thing you can at this point is nothing. There will be an expectation in the organization that data and feedback are going to be used to drive positive change. There will be an appetite for change and improvement. If you implement the necessary change, your organization will reap the benefits of this investment. Like any other measurement data, people data needs to be brought to life and form the basis for action. This key message was emphasized already in the first chapter of the book, where the process from data to action is also outlined. In its simplest form, the "data to action" process consists of three steps:

1. Understand and make sense of the people data by yourself as an organization leader and together with your leadership team
2. Share reports and overviews with your team/the individual and through discussion and further analysis reach a common understanding on what the data tell us

3.   Act in terms of identifying, prioritizing, and managing change actions the SMART way.[1]

The present chapter will provide details on how you apply human capital metrics to drive change in your company. This phase is called the "data to action" or "post-data" process. I will use a worked process around employee engagement and engaging leadership to exemplify how this can be done. The chapter also includes guidance on how to track progress on actions and how to keep the post-data process alive between measurement periods.

Measure to manage

As the management adage goes, "You can't manage what you don't measure." Without human capital metrics, you will never know if your people actions maintain the status quo or make things better or worse. With your metrics in place, you manage for improvement by monitoring what is getting better and what is not.

But how do you measure to manage? As we have seen in the previous chapters, the first imperative is to measure what is important. Less is often more. When you have a whole lot of metrics that are considered to be important for effective people management, it becomes more difficult to pinpoint which ones really matter. Manageable metrics are essential. Look at each of your metrics individually and judge if they can be managed in your company. One criterion for managing it is that leaders and managers can directly influence the metric by asking someone to do something differently and subsequently see the desired change in the metric (and workplace). When the metric is actionable and manageable, it has the potential to matter.

Another criterion is the way in which the metric supports action. Does it tell us something about the past or does it predict something about the future?

• Lagging indicators are metrics that measure end-state objectives or desired outcomes.

• Leading indicators are metrics that precede, anticipate, predict, or affect future desired outcomes.[2]

All financial metrics are lagging indicators. Human capital metrics can be both lagging and leading. As mentioned in Chapter 3, a high turn-over rate with many employees leaving your company may precede lower customer service scores as customers will experience old relation-ships being broken and new collaboration taking time to mature and become as intimate and effective as the past collaboration. Leading indi-cators are good because you have time to alter the course of your action or take a complete different direction. Leading indicators also establish urgency, as you will not have all the time in the world to amend things.

A big part of measure to manage is communication. It is important that you communicate your metrics both up and down the organiza-tion. Your manager wants to know what is going on and your employ-ees also need to know. No one is motivated to improve and change things unless they know how they are doing and where they are going. In addition, most of the suggestions on how to improve and change will come from employees and colleagues, so dialogue is needed. Publish your metrics and benchmarks, either online or by hanging charts on the wall, or both. Use pie charts, line charts, key driver charts, and other graphs to quickly, easily, and visually communicate the metrics. Review your metrics and use them to guide your deci-sions. With your metrics well communicated, you will get a broad and common understanding of which strategies are working and which are not. If you make a change, you use the metrics to tell you whether the change improved things or not. When the metrics show improve-ment, share that success with everyone. Tell your manager. Tell your staff. Reward people for exceeding their goals in public or one-on-one (depending on circumstances or preferences). Sometimes all you have to give is a verbal pat on the back.

And so the circle goes. Now you start over again. Is the metric important? Is it actionable and manageable, leading, or lagging? What is the urgency for action? How do I communicate metrics to all stakeholders? How do we change, and how do I reward the people who are responsible for success?

Post-data process

The post-data process or metrics follow-up is the management part where the majority of the company's time and energy should be consumed. A rule of thumb is that measuring human capital is 20% of the effort and managing human capital is the remaining 80%. The post-data process consists of the three steps as shown in the introduction to this chapter. In Table 6.1, you can see the range of activities involved in each of the steps.

Remember that you cannot take action on areas that are outside your control (Table 6.1). That is why many organizations work with a hierarchy of actions, which specifies where (and with whom) in

Table 6.1   The post-data process where you manage your human capital

Step One: Understand	Step Two: Share	Step Three: Act
• You have your metrics at hand. • You take a moment to read and interpret them. • You form your own initial understanding. • You book a time with your manager to discuss with him/her. • If anything looks odd, you check the data findings with HR and validate against other sources.	• You distribute and communicate results as required. • If anything is difficult to communicate, run it by another manager, HR, or Communications to cover all perspectives. • You book one-on-one meetings and/or team workshops. • You prepare how you will present results in the meeting and generally facilitate the results-to-actions flow. • You may want to get an external facilitator for workshops so that you can participate on equal terms with the other participants. • At the end of the session, you have possible action alternatives documented.	• If the list of action alternatives is documented and accountabilities agreed, you move to action. • If further prioritization and allocation of roles and responsibilities are needed, you orchestrate this before moving to action. • Actions are carried out. • You monitor progress, celebrating improvements, opening new actions, and adjusting others. • You evaluate the metric follow-up process and give feedback on the quality of metrics and measuring process as well as to using and applying the metrics in the post-data phase.

the organization action accountability sits. We will look at action hierarchies and accountability matrixes in the worked examples in the following sections. Essentially, you define process, tools, and target of metrics follow-up individually for the different hierarchical levels of the organization such as company, business unit or country, and team. In this way, actions are aligned throughout the company to what can be mandated, controlled, and changed at the different levels. Actions are complementary. Actions help to create a sense of urgency, purpose, and excitement around improving and innovating the way we work, collaborate and compete. Actions keep the overall "measure to manage" process alive.

Remember, too, that consideration of alternatives before moving from analyses of metrics to decisions on actions will raise the level of impact. It is a common mistake to box yourself in with limited alternatives. There is limited time and we need to do something now. This is business as usual and there is no need to come up with alternative solutions. Are these constraints real or mental barriers? Sometimes the difficulty is not devising a range of alternatives, but creating win-win alternatives. Win-win actions address the objectives of several stakeholder groups simultaneous. Suppose you have decided to approach another manager to try to get one of her high-performing employees to move to your team. You both know that this employee is interested in a move. You discuss with HR and get an additional headcount approved for your team. You make an arrangement where the employee divides the time between the old department and your department until a new headcount is on board with your colleague's team. A win-win alternative is satisfying for all.

Go or no go for employee engagement at your company

Suppose you do not have an employee engagement process or engagement metrics in place for your company. You keep hearing from leaders of other companies within your network as well as managers joining your company that employee engagement is important for performance and innovation capabilities. A dialogue platform where all teams and employees share and act on feedback about important aspects of the company and workplace creates purpose and competitive edge.[3]

Before making a decision to introduce an employee engagement program at your company, you would like to explore a little deeper why engagement is important, what it actually is all about, and how a process could possibly run within your workplace.

The "why" of employee engagement

The employee engagement process is a dialogue platform where leaders, experts, and workers voice their opinions and feedback is used to drive change. Simply having a voice builds loyalty to the organization in my experience.

The vision for employee engagement is to improve performance culture and organization health and as such engagement is important regardless of the size of your company. The first thing you do is to align this strategic concept of employee engagement to the people part of your corporate strategy. With empowered and committed people as a strategic lever, top management demonstrates that they are behind employee engagement. A tip is to showcase top management's commitment by collecting and communicating personal stories or quotes from the CEO (or fellow leaders) as part of the reasons why employee engagement makes a difference at your company. You find some examples of quotes for inspiration in Figure 6.1.

As it is also discussed in the earlier Chapters 1 and 2 of this book, a people strategy as part of the overall business strategy supports execution and there is plenty of research that proves the link between high employee engagement and high performance (Figure 6.1). I prefer the way Gallup Q12 provides evidence for this relationship. Their research shows that companies with high engagement scores are not only up to 20% better performing in terms of customer loyalty, profitability, and productivity compared to those with low engagement. High

FIGURE 6.1 CEO/CXO quotes to show senior management's commitment to employee engagement

engagement also leads to a range of organization health benefits such as 40% fewer people being absent, 50% fewer accidents occurring, 60% less theft, 80% fewer people becoming depressed, and huge positive effects on general physical and mental health.[4]

In the 21st century, engaging leadership is wanted and required by managers and subordinates alike. Research from IBM, former Kenexa High Performance Institute, indicates that leaders who inspire, respect, and reward their people get up to three times more engagement.[5] Leaders are huge contributors in creating an engaging work environment. Employees who work for engaging leaders score 85% favorable on the employee engagement index compared with a 25% favorable score by employees who work for leaders who are not engaging. Subordinates want to follow engaging leaders. And leaders themselves increasingly demand to get feedback through an employee engagement process so that they will know their standing and how to develop and grow their leadership brand.

Do not forget that, apart from aspirations, employees have expectations and choices, too. We all expect to be able to participate in a quality dialogue on how it is to work here and how to be able to do the best work of our lives right here and right now. We all have choices and we can take the exit if it is not possible to have a voice and a say about improving and innovating the way we work, collaborate, and compete.

The "what" of employee engagement

You will want to define what engagement is for your company. A definition that fits you exactly is useful for everyone who is going to be occupied with the process (which is most of the company, in fact). Engagement is a fancy word until you define it and make it relevant for your organization. Some people say about engagement that you know it when you see it. If you think about a work experience where you felt fully engaged, what words come to mind? The words you recall are probably included in the following bullet points describing engaged employees:

- Feel more fulfilled
- Want to go the extra mile
- Are more self-motivated and constantly develop
- Embrace change and make it happen
- Raise the bar and do better
- Create a winning culture that attracts and retains great people
- Build organizational citizenship and cares about their company being an awesome place to work

One definition of engagement can be along the lines: "It's about how motivated we are to contribute to and stay with this organization."

You can have high engagement without high performance and you can have high performance without high engagement. To support sustainable growth, however, you need both high engagement and high performance. Table 6.2 shows the interplay of engagement and performance. There are two metrics capturing levels of engagement and performance, respectively. Units and teams can be plotted onto the matrix. In the top right-hand quadrant, employees are both highly engaged and highly performing, fully aligned with the business strategy and customers and fully enabled by organization values, processes, and tools.

Table 6.2   Interplay of engagement and performance where you want to aim for high engagement AND high performance as in the top right-hand box

Interplay of Engagement and Performance	Low Performance	High Performance
High Engagement	**Reinventing the wheel** Employees' passion is not leveraged. Employees are aligned but not enabled. Focus needs to be on processes and infrastructure.	**Firing on all cylinders** Employees think and act like customers. They are aligned to vision and mission and enabled by organization culture, processes, and tools. Focus needs to be on sustaining the balance.
Low Engagement	**Broken bureaucracy** Employees are overwhelmed. No alignment and no enablement happen. Focus needs to be on kick-starting employee energy and driving performance.	**Process-driven organization** Employees act like zombies. Employees are enabled but not aligned. Focus needs to be on purpose, culture, and values to re-create passion and retain top talent.

You may ask if engagement is just another term for job satisfaction. Engagement is actually more than being satisfied with and in the job. To be engaged, you feel aligned with the company purpose and vision and are enabled by processes and opportunities to execute your job in the best way. To be satisfied does not require you to be aligned and/ or enabled. You are content but not necessarily excited, passionate, or happy about what you do. Engagement is a prerequisite for extraordinary performance. The opposite of being engaged is to be burned out, where the employee misses direction, lacks job resources, cannot see how he or she contributes, and feels tired or even sad.

What do people give you in return for their salary? What proportion of the human capabilities of your workforce are you getting? Gary Hamel, a visiting professor at the London Business School, talks about the pyramid of human capabilities.[6] If people are disengaged, they will perhaps just give you obedience, show up, follow the guidelines, do

Table 6.3   Accountability matrix with roles and responsibilities for employee engagement in the full organization

Employees	• Participate in surveys, give honest feedback. • Actively discuss and agree on action planning on results. • Take ownership of some of the team's action items. • Actively engage in follow-up activities and making their team, and the company in general, an awesome place to work. • Remember you are responsible for the wellbeing of your peers—your role is bigger than the job.
Line Managers	• Share and discuss survey results in action-planning sessions. • Identify, together with the team, relevant priorities for action. • Implement, monitor, and update action points. • Reflect on own capability to manage engagement, as typically measured by the Manager Effectiveness Index (as part of the Standard Human Capital Metrics Toolbox).
Functional Leaders	• Share and discuss survey results in action-planning sessions for whole function. • Identify relevant priorities for action. • Implement, monitor and update action points. • Hold line managers in unit accountable for doing the same. • Reflect on own and unit leadership, how engaging is this perceived to be?
Senior Management	• Listen to—and try to resolve—issues which have been fed upwards. • Take responsibility for survey results and your strategic response. • Reflect and act on Senior Management/company level areas. • Place survey results as a standard agenda item for leadership team meetings—discuss progress and commitment. • Walk the talk!
HR	• Be "experts" on employee engagement and give support to follow-up process, e.g. facilitating workshops. • Support and challenge line managers/functional leaders to improve their engagement. • Remind leaders and managers of the importance of communicating survey results and progress on actions to the organization/teams. • Be aware of and share Best Practice within the company.

the job and leave as early as possible. On the other hand, they will not require much more than a salary. If people are engaged, they will bring their initiative, imagination, and passion, but they will also want more than a salary in return. They will want meaning, intellectually and spiritually from work! You raise the bar from using people as commodities to having employees who create value and engagement in your work environment and for your customers.

The "how" of employee engagement

In Chapter 5 when discussing the standard toolbox, I talked about accountability for talent management and how we are all accountable in different ways for measuring and managing talent in the company. We can extend this framework to employee engagement. "I love my job" indicates that it starts with the individual employee or manager. Essentially, employee engagement is "I" X "the work environment." Roles and responsibilities in the organization around employee engagement can be illustrated by means of an accountability matrix, as shown in Table 6.3.

You use this matrix framework to fill in the relevant roles and activities in your company and, subsequently, to hold people accountable for playing their parts.

Yes, we go for employee engagement

We have now explored why engagement is important, what it actually is all about, and how an employee engagement process could possibly be executed within your company. Let us assume that you believe employee engagement is important for performance and innovation and that a regular dialogue around working here will create purpose and energy. You decide to go for it!

At this point, you will need to consider the modus operandi for employee engagement at your company. Will you run it in-house or will you source a supplier to administer the process for you? Whether you want external benchmarks for the survey items in your questionnaire will be one decision parameter. External benchmarks need to be sourced from outside. You license the question set from a supplier as part of the employee engagement consultancy and administration offered. Or you license the question set on its own for a specific license fee, though this is not very common.

The HR team would be in charge of collecting the business requirements for employee engagement and, together with IT and Sourcing, evaluate potential suppliers against the list of requirements through a Request for Proposal procedure. A supplier screening like the one in Table 6.4 may be handy for selecting the best supplier for you to partner up with. You group your requirements into themes, rate each theme on a 1 to 5 scale (where 5 is the best), add up the total score and provide explanatory comments.

Table 6.4   Framework for employee engagement research and survey supplier screening

Request for Proposal (RfP)	Supplier A	Supplier B	Supplier C
Can we work with this supplier team	4	4	3
Survey development and thought leadership	5	4	3
Survey administration and Information Technology	5	5	3
Integrating historical data	5	5	3
Reporting and analysis	5	4	2
Data action-planning support	4	3	2
Quality assurance	5	5	4
What do you think? Tell us what we don't know! In the light of the company description, how would you manage employee engagement and surveying?	5	3	1
Total score (40 points possible)	38	33	21
Comments	Inspiring RfP. Excellent benchmarks. Thought leadership.	Good industry representation. Main competitors use this vendor.	Overall poor performance. No relevant track record. Experiences from irrelevant industries.

A supplier selection procedure would involve suppliers responding to your business requirements in your Request for Information and Request for Proposal, beauty parades where the suppliers present their team and solution, an e-auction to get price visibility and cut costs, and final contract negotiation.

Employee engagement: questionnaire and reports

As mentioned earlier, employee engagement is measured by means of a survey. It is essential that you get concise, relevant, and actionable questions for your company included in the survey questionnaire. In an employee engagement process, the entire organization gets to work with two constructs, namely the survey questionnaire and the survey reports. These two constructs are paramount. You want your survey questionnaire to measure organization processes and competences that are strategic, aspirational, and forward-looking for your company. Organization processes and competences can be divided into five categories or themes influencing employee engagement. These are the work, the team, the manager, the customers and the company. Here are some examples of forward-looking and actionable question statements grouped according to these basic themes, which I have in fact licensed and used successfully over the past decade (in many variations and with different wordings):

- Work
    - I am appropriately involved in decisions that affect my work.
    - I have access to the information and equipment I need to do my work effectively.
    - My job makes good use of my knowledge, skills, and abilities.
    - This company provides me with the opportunity for learning and development.
    - In this company people are rewarded according to their job performance.
- Team
    - I feel my colleagues do quality work every day.
    - In my team you can feel high energy and excitement.
    - In my team we regularly use customer feedback to improve what we do.
    - In my team working together is encouraged.

- Manager
  - My manager encourages my development at work.
  - My manager treats me with respect.
  - My manager supports execution of the strategy effectively.
  - My manager inspires the best in people.
- Customers
  - This company is quick to adapt to changing customer demands.
  - Senior management is committed to providing high quality products and services to external customers.
  - As a customer of this company, I would be extremely satisfied with the quality of the products and services I receive.
- Company
  - Senior Management has communicated a vision of the future that motivates me.
  - I have confidence in the leadership ability of Senior Management.
  - At this company we live and breathe our values.

The objective is to secure concise, relevant, and actionable survey items and make the questionnaire proprietary to your workplace.

As for survey reports, they will naturally show responses to the questions asked in the survey. A quick turn-around of metrics from survey administration to report opening is essential as you will want to look at relatively fresh data in your reports. In principle, results can be available as soon as the survey closes, if it is online only (no paper surveys). However, a window of minimum two weeks to check data quality and calculate internal benchmarks and other statistics is often required. The response rate reporting will actually open simultaneously with the survey as this is a simple overview of responses per organization units and teams and also typically distributed to a smaller audience across the organization.

Actions hierarchy

Earlier in this chapter, we touched upon the actions hierarchy specifying where (and with whom) in the organization action accountability sits. The actions hierarchy and the different calls to action on the data you require for successful change management will dictate your reporting needs. If you require action to be taken on organization level (whole company and P&L businesses) and on team level, you would need two types of reports: 1) executive summary reports for the whole company and the main business units and 2) manager reports for the divisions and teams. You would design templates for each type of report with each set of data supporting clear calls to action. You would work with a two-layered survey follow-up process as illustrated Table 6.5.

Building your reports so that they support appropriate calls to action is quite an art. I have often cooperated with colleagues in Finance, on the one hand, to make reports crisp and clear in terms of numbers and statistics, while, on the other, close collaboration with colleagues in Communications has secured crisp and clear messages and findings.

As a heads up or early warning to the organization around survey reporting, you can communicate the reporting cascade well in advance of results being published. The reporting cascade states when exactly what reports are being released and who is responsible for what. This is the date when preliminary results on company level will be available. Executive summary reports for full company and P&L businesses will

Table 6.5 Two-layered survey follow-up process

	Organization level	Team level
Process	Executive summary reports are shared with respective leadership teams. Company/P&L Business deep dive, discussion in leadership team, facilitated by Group HR. Strategic response is communicated. Action area(s) for whole company is stipulated.	Managers share results for team discussion and action planning, team executes action and monitors progress, celebrating closed actions and committing to new actions.
Target	Employee Engagement Index on recommendation and commitment to increase from one survey period to the next survey period.	Survey follow-up metric "My team has taken action based on feedback from the last survey" to be more than 50% favorable when introduced in next survey round.

be published. The online reporting tool will open for HR. And lastly, managers will receive their division and team reports. A reporting cascade also ensures that metrics are provided in an orderly manner. You will want the leadership team to know about the state of the nation before metrics on division and team level are distributed.

The three steps in the survey follow-up process

As demonstrated at the beginning of this chapter (please refer to Figure 6.1: The post-data process where you manage your human capital), the post-data process or, in this case, survey follow-up consists of the three steps of understanding, sharing, and acting on the people data results and findings. We will now have a detailed look at what each of these steps involves in practice.

Survey follow-up step one: Understand

Survey measures

The questions you ask in your survey will be your survey measures. You may distinguish between key metrics and other survey dimensions. Key metrics represent the areas where stakeholder groups can best influence and should direct action efforts. Key metrics are different at the organization level and team level to ensure action efforts across the company are complementary. Survey measures would typically include two of the 11 metrics from the Standard Human Capital Metrics Toolbox outlined earlier in Chapter 5, that is, the Employee Engagement Index (metric number 4 in the toolbox) and the Manager Effectiveness Index (metric number 5) (see Figure 6.2).

The boxes in Figure 6.2 show possible survey measures following the logic of the basic themes affecting employee engagement: Work, Team, Manager, Customers, and Company. Key metrics at team level may include work, team, and customers, where the team's calls to action should be directed. Key metrics at the organization level

Manager Effectiveness	Team
X items on respect, development, execution, and inspiration	*X items on quality focus, collaboration, and energy*

Employee Engagement
X items on pride, advocacy, and commitment

Customers	Company	Work
X items on organisation agility, quality focus, and satisfaction	*X items on vision, confidence in leadership, living values*	*X items on involvement, enablement, and reward*

FIGURE 6.2 Example of survey measures in your employee engagement survey

involve company and customers (plus anything else requiring a strategic response), and manager level call to action revolves around the Manager Effectiveness metric.

Interpreting employee engagement results

Let us continue with understanding and interpreting results:

• Response rates
• % Favorable absolute standings
• Average scores
• Relative comparisons against benchmarks and trend lines
• Engagement priorities.

Response rates matter! Very high (more than 85%) and high response rates (more than 70%) make results representative and significant. There is a high acceptance of the survey. At the same time, expectations of follow-up are very positive and the risks of disappointment extremely high. High response rates are a mandate for action! Be cautious, though, of artificially high response rates due to forced participation where results may be misleading. I have often witnessed managers competing for the highest response rate in their division, resulting in employees being bombarded with emails and requests to participate, which really works against the voluntary nature of the process. If managers should compete on anything, it should be the highest employee engagement score or manager effectiveness result. A response rate of less than 50% is low and indicates low acceptance of employee engagement and low expectation that feedback is used to drive change at the workplace.

In interpreting your metrics, you gradually build up your understanding by first looking at absolute scores, then relative comparisons, and finally engagement priorities.

Absolute standings provide general information about employee perceptions:

- 70% favorable or more is usually considered an absolute strength
- Less than 50% favorable is usually considered an absolute concern
- More than 25% unfavorable is often considered an absolute concern
- 25% neutral may represent a high level of uncertainty and/or lack of knowledge or strong opinion and is usually considered a potential slide area or opportunity to bring people into the favorable camp.

Percent favorable, neutral, and unfavorable scores are commonly used in the survey industry. It is based on the 5-point Likert response scale where a 1 rating is strongly disagreeing and a 5 rating is strongly agreeing. Strongly disagree and disagree responses are collapsed into % unfavorable, neither agree nor disagree into % neutral, and agree and strongly agree (ratings 4 and 5) into % favorable.

Relative comparisons bring meaning to % favorable scores. Typical scores fall within 50% to 70% favorable. How is my score relative to internal benchmarks like the overall company average or a company top 25%? How do I compare to external norms like a country or industry norm? How do I trend relative to previous survey results? Remember to consider sample size (n) when making comparisons. For very large groups (e.g. 1,000+), a difference of 2–3% points is significant, for large groups (e.g. 100+), this could be 5% points, while for smaller groups the difference should be even greater, for example, around 10% points for more than 50 respondents and 15% points for less than 50.

Building on absolute standings and relative comparisons, you now consider the value the individual survey item or survey index has for achieving the company's goals. What are the priority questions for Employee Engagement for your team? How do you score on them? How do the key indices score? Are there any aspects that could be built upon or improved?

Priority questions for Employee Engagement are the top ten survey items that have the strongest statistical link with Employee Engagement. Priorities are established through correlational analysis, a common statistical procedure for identifying factors that have a statistically strong relationship with a dependent variable, in this case, the Employee Engagement Index. A correlational coefficient, denoted by r, close to +1 indicates a perfect positive relationship. The engagement priority analysis and results help to pinpoint where you should focus action to improve engagement in your team.

Survey follow-up step two: Share

A certain rigor around survey follow-up is a good move and can be achieved by promoting and putting in place recommended activities and time lines for e.g. team level sharing and communicating of results. Within one month of receiving their reports, managers are expected to share a snapshot of the data with their teams as well as to schedule and conduct the first team workshop to communicate results and discuss and agree areas for action. Within two months of receiving reports, managers have facilitated a second team workshop to consolidate actions. If there is a dedicated action-planning tool, actions are logged here. If not, managers or their delegates document actions on their own initiative and according to the SMART (Specific, Measurable, Achievable, Realistic, and Time-bound) framework described in Chapter 3 of the book. The SMART action overview is shared with everyone in the team and, together with the engagement metrics for the team, posted on the walls of a common area, where everyone can see, reflect on, and hold each other accountable for progress. Within three months of receiving reports, teams are in action-mode, have started to do things differently, and revisit actions on a regular basis. After six months, teams may celebrate closed actions, start new actions, and adjust others as appropriate.

Workshops

To engage your team in the process requires dialogue, feedback, and ownership from all involved. Good preparation is important for involvement and participation. The results are a good starting point, but an open and constructive dialogue is needed in order to gain real commitment to change. The purpose of the workshop(s) is to position employee engagement in relation to your company's strategy and overall business, to review results and form a common understanding of the key findings, to brainstorm on a few focus areas that will have the biggest impact on performance, and to agree on how to keep the process of continuous feedback and follow-up alive. When getting ready to hold a workshop, you might consider the expectations the team might have, having enough time and a quiet location for a quality dialogue, and how to encourage all to participate and take ownership of the issues.

A 60-minute team workshop (or extend it if you think it is too compact) might happen as given in Table 6.6.

Table 6.6   Agenda for 60-minute team workshop for sharing results and agreeing action areas

Getting on the same page 0–15 minutes	• Manager presents team results and links to company people agenda. • Team discussion on results, is this in line with what we expected, any surprises?
What should change 15–30 minutes	• Depending on your team size, work in groups or pairs. • Select one question or topic that you think is most important. • Use the template (can be found below) to capture what we already do, what is missing, who should do what.
How do we execute 30–60 minutes	• Groups present their topic and what to do about it, capture topics on flipchart/screen. • Decide as a full team which two topics to take action on. • Use the actions already listed by the groups and add anything missing. • In the next workshop or regular team meeting, revisit and prioritize actions, and decide who does what and when, using the SMART approach to documenting actions and targeted improvements.

Using a template to capture what we already have (our strengths), what we could do better (our changes), and how each of us can support the changes (our actions) serves several purposes (see Figure 6.3).

The template illustrated in Figure 6.3 will help ensure that issues are recorded as they are highlighted, topically and truthfully. Attention is drawn to the questions and issues the team can control and influence. Focus stays on the positives, what we already have and how things can be just a little bit better with a few realistic tweaks. Accountability for change is highlighted. The work concludes with that paramount personal commitment to change—what do I commit to doing. Change happens one person at a time.

Another template that might be useful to highlight strengths and opportunities at the workshop is an action urgency and prioritization heat map (see Figure 6.4).

If you have an intelligent reporting and action-planning tool, this can be pre-populated for organizations and teams. On the other

---

Group Name: _____ Question/Focus Area: _____

1. **What is already there with the present score?** (What do we already have, say, hear, do with present score?)

2. **What is additionally there when it is a notch better?** (When it is better, something is different, "if only we had …, could do …, would hear …, saw …, could say ….")

3. **What is needed/what actions should be taken for being a notch better?**
   a) **What I want from the leadership team is …**
   b) **What I want from my manager is …**
   c) **What I want from my colleagues is …**
   d) **The things I want to do include …**

FIGURE 6.3 Template for capturing and committing to strengths, changes, and actions in groups/by individuals

Heat Map	Not engagement priorities but showing major opportunity	Among top 10 engagement priorities
Higher scores/above comparisons	**KEEP ON DOING THIS** My manager treats me with respect.	**BUILD ON THIS STRENGTH** Senior Management has communicated a vision of the future that motivates me.
Lower scores/below comparisons	In my team working together is encouraged. **WATCH THIS**	I am appropriately involved in decisions that affect my work. As a customer of this company, I would be extremely satisfied with the quality of the products and services I receive. **ACT IMMEDIATELY**

FIGURE 6.4 Heat map identifying priorities for action planning

hand, there is valuable learning in talking together as a team about what action areas belong where and how urgently actions need to be established. Anything in the quadrant for "Act Immediately" should be treated as the name indicates. In the above heat map example (Figure 6.4), the challenges that should be addressed immediately are "involvement in decisions" and "employees as ambassadors."

Conducting a quality dialogue on employees as ambassadors is invigorating and would also serve as a team building exercise. You could dedicate part of a regular team meeting to this discussion. What are the key factors about the company's international and local brands that you are proud of? What is each team member's favorite product from the company's portfolio? Why is this a favorite? Do you have any special stories to share around great moments as a customer of this product? How do family and friends perceive our products/services portfolio? Is anything missing? How can we improve relative to competition?

Survey follow-up step three: Act

Once you have identified the most important areas to focus, the next step is to (re-)prioritize, plan, and take action. Remember the basics:

- Keep it simple. Do not try to change everything; just aim to do a couple of things really well.
- Be specific and target action upon issues you can easily influence.
- Consider alternatives. Can constraints be alleviated? Win-win scenarios.
- Outline what success will look like and when you expect it to be achieved.
- Assign responsibility for the action. Encourage team involvement and individual accountability for change. This is not about the manager doing it all alone.
- Monitor progress. Revisit your action plan regularly and put it on your team meeting agenda once a month. Celebrate success and keep building momentum!

It is very useful to include questions on survey follow-up in the employee engagement program. First of all, it sends a signal to leaders and teams that the company is adamant that the end goal is action, not merely data. Second, the survey follow-up metrics can be used to monitor and incentivize the ways in which leaders and teams execute the post-data process. You would typically have a couple of questions on survey follow-up, e.g. "My team has taken action based on feedback from the last survey" and "Senior Management has taken action based on feedback from the last survey." Managing engagement, relative to measuring engagement, is one area where many companies are weak. The external average norm for survey follow-up is around 50% favorable, which means that only half of employees generally experience behavior change to take place after a survey has been conducted. If your company becomes a high performer on engagement management—with higher than external benchmark scores on survey follow-up capability—you will be quite unique!

Independent research[7] proves an increasing strength of relationship between engagement and survey follow-up. The increase goes from discussing results (I was given the opportunity to discuss my questions and ideas about the results of the previous Employee Engagement survey), through creating action plans (my team/division used the feedback from the previous Employee Engagement survey to create action plans), to following through (my team/division has implemented the action plan and continues to work toward our goals based on the feedback received from the previous Employee Engagement survey).

In essence, not sharing the feedback is not the most destructive thing you can do for your survey program. Instead, sharing feedback but not taking action is the most destructive thing you can do.

sharing feedback but not taking action is the most destructive thing you can do

Taking right action by right stakeholder from right data

The following is another real-life example of how leaders and managers might be inspired to take accountability for action priorities. The top ten company-wide drivers of engagement are established through correlational analysis. The logic behind engagement priorities is that action taken on any one of these questions is likely to drive the biggest change in engagement. Some leaders and managers are skeptical. How convinced are we about this statistics? How can we validate findings? Further analysis in the form of step-wise regression and discriminant analysis upon the company-wide priorities indeed confirm that each of the ten items is not only a driver, but, in fact, a strong predictor of engagement. People analytics seem to work and leaders across the organization do well to focus upon at least one of these ten things in their action plans to improve engagement. Leaders should focus on those items that they can most easily influence. These will be different depending on the organization level and, accordingly, the ten priorities for action must be divided into three clusters of engagement drivers requiring focus from senior management, local-level managers, and focus for all leaders. A catalogue of action ideas for each focus cluster provides inspiration all round:

- Focus for senior leadership
    - Inspiring confidence
    - Communicating a compelling vision of the future
    - Demonstrating employee wellbeing is important.
- Focus for local-level managers
    - Enabling employees to achieve their career goals
    - Enthusing their teams about the work and the company
    - Facilitating employee learning and development.
- Focus for all leaders
    - Hiring top talent
    - Retaining top talent
    - Delighting customers.

Applying people data and analytics to gain the attention of leaders and managers and to inspire and focus people's actions across the entire company creates a new (and sometimes needed) buzz around employee engagement.

Tracking progress

During the understand—share—act survey follow-up process, you will produce various documents on team strength and weaknesses, focus areas for improvement, priorities by groups and individuals, heat mapping and SMART targets and actions. This documentation becomes your baseline. At regular intervals, you should revisit this baseline documentation to monitor how you are progressing.

Formulating a "chance manifesto" might also support urgency and call to action. Something like:

> Our target is to drive behavioral change in the division toward a culture of mastery through working with leadership teams, delivery teams, and consumers. By the end of 20XX, we expect to see 1)

greater accountability, e.g. more prototyping, taking decisions where the relevant expertise is, clear escalation process, leaders not becoming bottlenecks, and embedding an expert growth path and 2) greater empathy for employees and customers, e.g. empowering employees, local decision power, catalogue of learning opportunities, focus on talent, using customer feedback to drive innovation, and avoiding "not invented here" and "silo thinking."

A common way to track progress is to use one of the employee engagement survey questions. For the change manifesto in the previous paragraph, this could be the item "This company provides me with the opportunity for learning and development" for the accountability part and the item "In my team we regularly use customer feedback to improve what we do" for the empathy part.

The gap-closure method is a fair way of setting improvement targets as it takes into account where you currently are relative to a (stretch) benchmark. The benchmark should be both aspirational and achievable and the company top 25% fits well with these two criteria. The gap-closure method is illustrated in Table 6.7.

Looking at Table 6.7, the gap between the current % favorable score and the company top 25% benchmark (or another relevant stretch norm) is calculated and a gap-closing target is set. We have here decided that we

Table 6.7　Gap-closure method for setting improvement targets

Gap-Closure Area	Current % favorable	Gap to company top 25%	Closing gap with 10%	Target for next measurement round
This company provides me with the opportunity for learning and development.	70	15	1.5	**72**
In my team we regularly use customer feedback to improve what we do	60	30	3.0	**63**

want to close the gap with 10% every survey period. The improvement target—or target for next survey in the figure—is the gap-closure percentage points added to your current score. You can set the gap-closure target to exactly as big as you prefer, though be aware of the time period you want to achieve this within. Setting a big gap closure for a limited time period makes it too aspirational and not achievable.

You might want to use a combination of company-wide and individual team or manager improvement targets. This was illustrated earlier in the chapter by the two-layered survey follow-up approach (Table 6.5). There are different calls to action on organization level and team level, respectively, which are supported by specific reporting, process, and improvement targets. Using specific improvement targets across the company for divisions and teams is an effective and fair way of driving behavioral change. The key is to keep the process tracking simple and not have to juggle with too many complicated and complementary targets. Target calculation and fulfillment should not overshadow the action itself, but merely support it.

Keeping it alive

Keeping change actions alive between measurement points is tricky. It is easy to lose the momentum, forget the call to action, and fall back on old habits and established ways of working. Some of the things you can do to keep up momentum are:

- Using regular measurements to guide direction and discipline around change actions.
- Continuous communication of change initiatives coming out of people data.
- Keep focusing on the essentials, adjusting and reducing the whole process to stay fresh and manageable.

Regular measurement

Regular measurement helps to keep focus on change direction, doing actions, and a disciplined approach. When employee engagement is part of executing your strategy, you will want to run a full survey once a year and possible a pulse check six months after to give you two measurement points annually. In the companies where I have previously worked, two annual measurement points have been in use and aligned with the performance management process. Employee engagement data feeds into mid-year and end-of-year performance dialogues and ratings.

Communicate, communicate, communicate

Communications around results and actions represents another area that is key for keeping the post-data process alive. The communications may flow according to the two-layered follow-up approach, with a communications plan for the full organization and communications advice for managers targeted at the team level. Communication elements would include:

- For *the understanding phase*, a thank you for participation with information on response rates and recap of next steps, i.e. when reports come out and what managers are supposed to do. Brief on top line results for the company/division and issue invitations to the results sharing and action-planning workshops.
- For *the sharing phase*, communications of engagement priorities and focus areas for action on organization level (by the Communications function) and team level (by the manager). Online forum for leaders and managers where engagement stories and interventions that work well for them are shared. Communication of best practices and proven interventions.
- For *the acting phase*, monthly news on progress on engagement priorities and action focus areas. Dialogues in company social media, i.e. how employees see progress, what they are missing, what we should do more of, facilitated by the HR and Communications functions in cooperation.

Focus and simplify all the while

Where many businesses and teams fail is when they try to take on too much. It can be either a very complicated survey administration with too many and not actionable questions resulting in messy reporting without a clear call to action or divisions and teams being overconfident about their change capabilities and pursuing everything without direction and discipline. My experience with employee engagement is that you need to purposefully, deliberately, and strategically eliminate the non-essentials and constantly keep reducing, focusing, and simplifying to keep it fresh and relevant. This is more easily said than done in an organizational setting; however, it characterizes successful leaders, teams, organizations—and processes.

The following two chapters will focus on the most common limitations, obstacles, and types of skepticism to be encountered and how to overcome them. This involves both process issues and psychological barriers. Chapter 7 is about limitations and obstacles and Chapter 8 introduces a number of real-life skeptics and what can be done around "metrics for skeptics."

chapter 1

Limitations and Obstacles

The whole book has been about how to think, analyze and act systematically around human capital metrics so that you will be better prepared to work with people data and make data-driven people decisions. Along the way, I have explored the difficulties, conflicts, and constraints involved in this process. In this chapter, I will summarize the most common limitations and obstacles to be encountered and suggest how you might overcome them.

From my experience the limitations and obstacles to using metrics tend to be based on both process issues and psychological barriers or some combination of both. You will no doubt find that while some limitations and obstacles are obvious and visible, others are irrational and invisible. For example, you will spot an incorrect percentage or other calculation, which is easy to sort out, once it is found, however, you may also need to acknowledge and confront your own reaction to or even denial of a poor result. The list below provides you with a summary of the most common limitations and obstacles:

- Availability and quality of data
- Ambition level and organization maturity
- Resistance to measurement
- Inability to work with the metrics
- Inability to take action from people data
- Lack of feedback facilitation skills

- Resistance to data-driven people management and change
- Missing accountability in the organization
- Balancing analytical and action-oriented.

By familiarizing yourself with potential process mistakes and typical psychological barriers, I believe you will be better able to read and use people data critically and objectively and ensure your people decisions are sound and reliable.

Looking at availability and quality of data

As discussed earlier, availability and quality of data are essential characteristics that determine access to and reliability of people data for making decisions. Availability and quality mean accessibility on demand, reliability, readability, and actionableness. In other words, your people data is easy to get to, easy to trust, easy to understand, and easy to take action from.

The availability of human capital metrics depends on the processes and tools you have in place at your company. For the 11 human capital metrics in the Standard Toolbox in Chapter 5, I outlined typical data sources and shared with you ideas as to how you can keep your own records, in case you cannot get the data from a common standard business system.

Availability of human capital metrics is a bigger issue than data quality for managers. Once available, people data in business systems is likely to be of good quality and actionable because of the growth in both professional talent management solutions and people analytics capabilities in HR in recent years. The bottom-line is that you as a manager are totally dependent on your company's investment in talent management resources, be they HR staff, processes, or software.

Overcoming limitations and obstacles

- Start to require reliable people data to be available at your fingertips. You want numbers, benchmarks, and facts to support you on people decisions, just as you have it for other business decisions like marketing, IT, and supply chain.

- Underline the urgency for your organization. If competitors are moving forward with Big Data, we should too. We might start by putting in place a strong foundation for managing data quality with best-in-class data quality practices and tools.
- Build the business case with arguments from the early chapters of this book: Why Bother about Human Capital Metrics (Chapter 1) and Working Strategically with Human Capital (Chapter 2).
- Ask HR and IT to scan the market for talent management solutions. You can use 11 talent management metrics in the Standard Toolbox as your minimum requirements for a solution.

Eating the elephant one piece at a time

In Chapter 2 I discussed how usage of human capital metrics depends on organization maturity. There are three maturity levels for organizations; they can be (1) immature, (2) aspirational, or (3) mature. Each and every organization will be at its own unique starting point, which will dictate its choices. Being unrealistic about where you are, where you want to go, and at which pace will make your journey much more painful and costly.

Being overconfident of own implementation capability and scoping too big a project are the most common mistakes. "Eating the elephant one piece at a time" will ensure that the selected process works end-to-end and reliable data and actionable statistics are available for the right stakeholders at the right time.

Overcoming limitations and obstacles

- Be realistic about how your company can cope with human capital metrics. Accept where you are and make a solid plan of where you want to go and how to get there.
- Start small by concentrating on one part—your high-ROI people activities—of the employee life cycle. Employee engagement is a

good example because of the proven link to business performance and organization health. Become a champion on turning data into action on your selected process. Then scale up by adding more processes, one at a time.

• Be adamant about the post-data process where leaders and teams should spend 80% of their efforts driving the change they want to see and where the company will become a winner in the marketplace.

Resistance to measurement

Mathematics is perhaps the school subject that mostly divides students. We either love it or hate it. The majority of students fall into the hate group. Sometimes this is because of bad teaching or because we believe we suffer from dyscalculia, the fear that we cannot acquire arithmetical skills.

Human capital metrics, statistics, people analytics, drivers, predictors, big data, does it get any worse? Resistance to measurement is deeply inherent in us and fosters disbelief and distrust toward the entire measurement process. It can be expressed in many different ways from "you don't understand what I am doing" to "my work is too important to be measured." The one case about fudging the numbers gets blown out of proportion. The rare case about wrong data being used for making a bad decision is the one story being remembered and re-told. The untypical example of not communicating company results and shared outcomes damages reputation for years to come even after you get a good communications routine in place.

Overcoming limitations and obstacles

• Refrain from overcomplicating it. Make it just as exclusive as it has to be. You do not need a degree in statistics, but can use your school math.
• Select metrics that are relevant for the business and can be used to drive change.
• Communicate timely and honestly about the why, what, and how of people measurement and talent management.

- Provide training to the business and HR on how to interpret the measures, contextualize results, call to action, post-data process and follow-up.
- Be fully transparent about results, findings, and actions and publish it electronically and physically.

Inability to work with the metrics

Inability to work with the human capital metrics being used may be founded on missing interpretation skills, lack of understanding about the process and/or how to access results, seeing what you want to see, and difficulties dealing with poor and good results, respectively.

Not being able to interpret a measure and the meaning of results inhibits acting on results and effecting improvement. What do results mean? What is the story behind the data? How does it read in the business context? What impact does the metric have on human capital management?

Be careful not to selectively see what you want to see, give too much weight to evidence supporting your inclination, or dismiss conflicting information. Poor results are more difficult to accept and often lead to denial and mistrust. "These are not my results; they are erroneous, out of business context, the data administration process is faulty" are things you tend to hear when this is in play. On the other hand, very good results may lead to no perceived need for action as well as real issues not surfacing. In highly hierarchical organizations and cultures, we tend to see higher results, a bias which, of course, is also reflected in comparable norms and benchmarks. People in these organizations may be afraid of their boss and have little experience with an open feedback culture and speaking their mind.

Overcoming limitations and obstacles

- If your people data processes and tools are intuitive and supported by simple user guides, it is easy to learn by doing!

- Make sure to get the basics of what is being measured and what is required by you.
- Look for help. "Peter has been successful in this area. I wonder if he could give me a few pointers?" "I should probably go to that training next month." Provide advice from your own experience and recommend helpful resources to others.
- Enroll on the available training sessions where you can learn about the process of collecting, distributing, interpreting, and taking action on human capital metrics in your company. Make clear instructions on how reports differ, what is available, and how to access the different reports. Introduce the "Accountability Matrix" found in Chapter 6 (Table 6.3) illustrating roles and responsibilities of employees, line managers, functional leaders, senior management, and HR in creating an awesome place to work.
- Be honest with yourself about your motives. Are you just looking for evidence confirming what you think you see and would like to do? It is a natural tendency to be more engaged by what we like than by what we dislike. In sharing and discussing results with individuals or teams, refrain from asking leading questions that invite confirming evidence and make sure conflicting information is examined as rigorously. A leading question might be "You gave a score of 3 on this question, didn't you?" A non-leading question might be "What should we do to improve the score of 3 on this question?" or "How come we have a score of 3 on this and a score of 5 on that?"
- With poor results, accept this is only one data point that must be read in context. It is the subsequent dialogue and action that lead to change and growth. Be aware of common reactions to poor results such as shock, anger, and rejection. We are often unaware of how others see us, so leaders and managers may be surprised and momentarily shocked when they see data they did not expect. A typical response to an employee engagement survey is "How could my team say this about me?" Any form of implied criticism in the way that people see us can be disturbing, even though we may end up agreeing with it. "They don't know the real me. And besides, I'm doing OK anyway." Often it is tempting for leaders and

managers to put the data aside to avoid dealing with it. Be open-minded and find your inner curiosity. Conflicts and counterarguments may actually lead to better outcomes. It is not personal, but about the business. Encourage objective interpretation. Why might the scores be so? See data as representative of a team and refrain from trying to identify individual responses. Remember to focus on strengths as well as weaknesses.

- Be inspired by good results. Always be hungry for change because you can always improve. Remember that results not addressed tend to decline year on year so your positive good results will not remain good if no action is taken. Become a case of best practice in the business. A non-hierarchical culture allows staff to continually ask questions of all leaders. Being listened to gives a feeling of being valued, which is the best way of keeping a workforce happy.

Inability to take action from people data

Reasons behind inability to take action based on the available people data may revolve around perceived lack of time, conflict with other organizational priorities, virtual team issues, and actions not recorded properly or being DUMB, not SMART.

Perceived lack of time is probably the reason for not taking action on people data that I have heard the most times. "I am too busy with running this program," "My travel schedule is too heavy over the next months," "I am with customers," and so forth. Being a prudent time manager (with all that it takes such as delegating and prioritizing) is part of effective leadership. Pressure from other organizational priorities is a common obstacle as well. It is interesting how people issues always seem to be at the bottom of the agenda! At the same time it is equally interesting how CEOs are always looking for increased engagement and ways to encourage employees to use more discretionary effort. Next time you are in a leadership team meeting, check it out for yourself. The people areas will most likely come last, after business updates and issues, just before AOB (Any Other Business). If like most people you always run late with your meetings, you never come to deal with the people areas.

A virtual team is a group where the members work across time, space, and organizational boundaries.[1] A virtual team is also known as a distributed team or remote team. Virtual team issues represent practical obstacles and collaborative limitations around trying to get to a shared understanding, harvesting improvement ideas, and moving forward with actions all can commit to. Even with enabling technology, video conferencing meeting rooms in all locations, you will struggle with different time zones and virtual facilitation of group work. Cost focus on traveling, introduced during the financial crisis but here to stay in most organizations, makes virtual team facilitation and collaboration necessary skills.

Finally, an inability to take action may relate to actions not being recorded properly. DUMB actions are dull, unclear, mundane, and boring. SMART actions are Specific, Measurable, Achievable, Realistic, and Time-bound. SMART versus DUMB targets are discussed in more detail in Chapter 3.

Overcoming limitations and obstacles

- Position people data as a lever for performance. High people results mean high business performance. Underline the role of effective leadership in managing talent. What can the manager do to free-up time to be a leader? Are you micromanaging? Are you spending too much time on tactical and operational problems as opposed to more strategic issues?
- With respect to conflicts with other organizational priorities, incorporate people findings and actions into existing plans and objectives. Remember the statement that "culture eats strategy for breakfast".[2] Challenge leaders and teams on how the action can best address their results. Have they focused on the most important issues to get the best value from action? Utilize the post-data process of understanding, sharing, and acting on results. This will save time and focus efforts on outcomes.
- In dealing with distributed team limitations, be sure to share results with all team members, not only with colleagues that are in the

same location as you. Reemphasize the right of every employee to receive feedback on results. Investigate alternative ways to generate discussion among remote team members: email, phone, videoconference, and delayed face-to-face meetings. Use a mixture of working together as a whole team with videoconferencing and groups collaborating face-to-face in locations. Utilize internal social media such as Socialcast, discussion boards, and intranet.

- With DUMB actions versus SMART actions, be aware of an overly simplistic focus, e.g. "increasing the employee engagement score." Actions should target aspirational, yet achievable outcomes. How can actions and targets be SMART, not DUMB? What will the team actually do to drive engagement? How will we measure success?
- Use reverse brainstorming to release humor and creativity in developing SMART actions. Begin with the DUMB actions. How do we make employees more dissatisfied? How do we reward poor performance? Then reverse actions and targets to become positives and SMART.
- Be aware that actions plans targeting too many issues, leaders assuming all responsibility, and/or actions targeted at others are not SMART. Reprioritize how and when we aim to achieve what. Reemphasize the importance of team ownership and accountability. Action planned by the team is likely to be recognized by it as more effective. Challenge the team as to how they can best influence and measure change. What actions are more specifically within their sphere of influence and what actions should be delegated up or down the organization?
- Using the template as illustrated in Figure 6.3 in Chapter 6, each individual commits to one or two tasks or change actions, which may then become part of the individual's performance objectives for the period.

Lack of feedback facilitation skills

Feedback facilitation skills cover a broad range of competences and actions:

- Workshop preparation, agenda, objectives, pre-reads
- Workshop execution

- Keeping time
- Getting everyone involved and not letting the conversation be dominated by just one or two people
- Take care not to solely focus on numbers at the expense of themes or a story
- Action planning and commitment to action
- Being realistic about how much the group can take on, being sufficiently specific
- Making sure targeted improvements are inside of the group's control.

Feedback facilitation is quite comprehensive and requires practice. You may try to avoid it and, consciously or unconsciously, but wrongly, hedge your exposure to those precious practice situations. There is also a range of different people data feedback situations such as:

- Ad-hoc versus scheduled
- One-on-one discussions
- Team meetings
- Bigger group workshops.

Lack of manager confidence with feedback facilitation is an issue to tackle in using and applying people data. First of all, people data is often pointing at what leaders and managers do well and less well. Receiving feedback is hard. The process strikes at the tension between two basic human needs, the need to learn and grow, and the need to be accepted just the way you are. Disregarding valuable feedback or, just as damaging, accepting and acting on feedback that you would be better off disregarding are equally tempting. When leaders act as feedback facilitators, you may feel tempted to do all the talking, be overcritical of the people data and methodology to the point of rejection, or come to the meeting with a prepared action plan. After all, "I'm in charge here."

Overcoming limitations and obstacles

- Taking feedback well is a bit like a filtering and sorting process. Filter through your feedback response patterns. Think through how easily you manage to receive feedback. Do you tend to reject feedback at first and then find it valid after reconsidering? Do you tend to accept feedback immediately and then later decide it is not valid? Do you tend to agree with it in theory, but not change anything in practice?

- Separate the "what" from the "who" and avoid shooting the messenger. I would personally have been dead many times over as the messenger of organizational ills having to give feedback that people did not want to hear!

- Sort toward coaching in your feedback approach. Some feedback is evaluative: "Your rating is a 4." Some feedback is coaching: "Here's how you can improve." It can be difficult to distinguish the two. So coach for performance more than provide evaluation.

- When you, in your leader role, act as feedback facilitator, try to forget your managerial status. Apply the 80/20 rule with the team talking 80% of the time and you, the leader, 20% of the time. Set expectations at the outset that everyone should contribute. Ask open questions. Invite contributions from the quieter individuals. Do not be afraid to challenge more vocal individuals to allow others to speak. You may want to get help from a professional facilitator from HR or externally and you can act in your normal role during the meeting.

- In overcoming obstacles in the feedback *preparation* phase, be sure to share results with all team members, not only those who are in the same location as you. Emphasize the right of every employee to receive feedback on results. Investigate alternative ways to generate discussion among remote team members—email, blog, phone, videoconference, or delayed face-to-face meetings. Send out invitations well in advance and include an exciting call to action. Build on the momentum of turning fresh data into real change.

- In overcoming obstacles in the feedback *execution* phase, stick to the planned circulated agenda and timelines. One meeting objective should be to generate constructive ways to address issues. Test whether or not the team agrees with the results during the feedback meeting. Continually take a step back and summarize if the team becomes too obsessed by detail. Balance discussion on both positives and negatives in order to avoid ending up without any suggestions for improvement. Set the expectation that at least one headline should be a strength area.

- In overcoming obstacles in the feedback *action-planning* phase, consider that the most important part of action planning is team contribution and ownership. If real ownership does not exist, the action plan may not address the most essential issues for the team. Aim for the team to agree upon 3–5 headlines by the end of the meeting. Use the timelines to stay focused. Embed people actions within the business plans.

The status quo trap

Applying people data means examining decision alternatives and planning action courses. The comfort of the status quo makes moving from data to action challenging. We are biased toward alternatives that perpetuate the current situation. This is what we know how to do. Think about product development. The first cars were called "horseless carriages." The newspapers we read on the web still today look very much like the printed versions. We have to fight to get out of our comfort zone and avoid the decisions and the actions that will not change the status quo. Sometimes maintaining the status quo may be the best choice, however, in working with human capital metrics, the end goal is change of some magnitude. Like Winston Churchill said, "To improve is to change, to be perfect is to change often."

To improve is to change, to be perfect is to change often

The first step toward change is awareness, which is what your human capital metrics bring. The second step is acceptance, which is what you bring. It is about the head and the heart. To change successfully, people need to be able to both think and feel positively about what we need to do. Without addressing both sides, change is less likely to occur. Kotter's eight steps of change are often used for major changes in the organization.[3] However, you may also find it useful on a smaller scale to avoid the status quo trap by providing a solid bridge to the future. Kotter's eight steps are:

1. Establish the sense of urgency
2. Build the guiding team
3. Get the right vision
4. Communicate for buy-in
5. Empower broad-based action
6. Create short-term wins
7. Consolidate gains
8. Make it stick.

Part of holding on to the status quo may be your desire to protect earlier decisions and any sunk costs involved. "Sunk costs" are related to previous investments of time and money that are now unrecoverable. Protecting earlier decisions is desirable when you were the one who made them. We all have a desire to be right! Therefore, you may prefer to keep that poor decision of the past hidden. Assume you want to fire a poorly performing new hire in your team; this means you will go public with your poor recruitment judgment. Perhaps it is safer to let the person stay on, even though it only magnifies the damage.

Overcoming limitations and obstacles

- Change before you have to. When you use metrics as leading indicators, you will understand in advance what changes are needed and have a limited time window to act within.
- Ask yourself whether you would choose the status quo alternative, if, in fact, it was not the status quo. Put the status quo to a test. Compare the status quo, as it would be, not as it is, with your other would-be alternatives. Think about if you joined this organization today, would you be happy with the status quo?
- Build on the status quo. Take the parts that work, identify your organization's strengths, and do incremental improvements. People change for something better, rather than to avoid something worse.

- Avoid exaggerating the time, effort, and cost involved in moving away from the status quo. Treat all alternatives, including the status quo, in the same way, carefully evaluating pluses and minuses.
- Communicate with what you *do*, not just what you say. Use simple language and avoid jargon and acronyms. Be sure to include the data appealing to people's heads and the stories from the data talking to people's hearts.
- Think about the old adage "If you find yourself in a hole, the best thing you can do is to stop digging." No decision maker is immune to errors in judgment. Admit to the mistake. Do the right thing; learn from it, and move on.
- Use Kotter's eight steps of change as your foundation. They will help you manage switching from the status quo by building the bridge to the future.
- Be ready to take one step back to go two steps forward. Expect some chaos. Be prepared to take a different track if things change or do not work.
- Not everyone "gets it" in the same way or in your timeframe. Welcome resistance. You are making progress! Be patient. People do not easily forget what they already know. They can take time to relearn.
- Do not over-rely on process or tools. Encourage quality dialogue and relationships.
- Seek expert help and support from your internal OD (Organization Development) function.

Missing accountability in the organization

The natural home in the organization for human capital metrics is the Human Resources (HR) function. People data is part of HR processes and tools. If HR does not lead the measurement effort, it will seriously limit your company's capability to use reliable people data to improve business performance and apply sound people actions to differentiate from competition. If HR conducts the measurement initiatives to produce HR statistics for their own functional needs and unrelated to the human capital measures needed by the business, it is equally limiting. If no one in the organization takes the lead on human capital metrics, the whole project will end up on the back burner.

It is important that HR collaborates with stakeholders within the business such as IT, Business Development, and Senior Management.

The HR function must collaborate with the IT function on tools and technology issues like infrastructure, security, access, testing of tools, handling of multiple languages, client-managed functionality, and helpdesk support. The IT function is also typically involved with interfaces and data feeds between the various IT systems.

The HR function could collaborate with the Business Development and Marketing functions to align people data requirements with strategic objectives, integrate people data with customer data, and learn from the mastery of analytics and big data existing in these other functions.

Senior Management is involved in giving the green light for the investment in talent management solutions. HR prepares and presents a business case on the basis of which Senior Management gives a go or no go.

Leaders and managers should be part of scoping, piloting, and testing the targeted metrics and tools. Intuitive and relevant talent management solutions help leaders and managers to not only make better people decisions, but also to up skill their own leadership and management competences. Ideally, leaders and managers would pull this process into the business, not, as it is usually the case, the HR function pushing it out into the organization.

Overcoming limitations and obstacles

- The HR function is encouraged by the business to sit in the driving seat for talent management solutions. Talent management is being pulled by the business rather than pushed by HR.
- HR collaborates with IT and Business Development to understand and document IT and business requirements for people data solutions.
- Make a compelling business case with an offer Senior Management cannot refuse.

- Pilot the solution in a critical and representative area of the business in order to get leaders' and managers' feedback, which can then be incorporated before full implementation.
- Cheer on leaders and managers to be proactive and demanding in measurement and management approaches to human capital.

Being analytical and/or action-oriented as the situation requires

As proposed in Chapter 1, the Plato statement of the unexamined (work) life not worth living is an apt mantra for companies pursuing and encouraging an analytical and evidence-driven culture. It is time to extend the analytical culture to talent management.

Suppose you find out from the employee engagement survey that one of your critical teams, consisting of one manager and ten team members, is currently totally disengaged. Their score has dropped like a stone since the last survey. The manager is the same and there have not been major changes in the team. However, less than a year ago, three new employees joined the team. Your first thought might be to move the manager. You also seem to recall some comments around this manager being quite tolerant of others' behavior. In any case, you decide to investigate a little on your own. You gather as many metrics as you can for the team, including diversity distribution, performance ratings of all individuals, employee engagement and manager effectiveness trends. You talk with HR about the data and any other inputs and observations for the team. You also decide to talk to one old team member and one new team member. You are still not wiser. Finally, you confront the manager. She is puzzled too, however, ahead of you, as she has just fired one of the new employees (not the one you spoke to) who clearly underperformed all along. She was too hesitant with this decision, had given this individual pet status out of misunderstood kindness, and the frustration with one individual had damaged the whole team in the end. The team would not give their manager away by talking to you as her manager, but they all independently of each other decided to give poor scores as a cry for help. This is an example of how an analytical culture means being analytical, action-oriented, and able to switch between analytical and action-oriented, as the situation requires—on part of both managers and employees.

The example also serves to illustrate how dangerously close we are to over relying on our initial thoughts. Your decision to move the manager would have been based on a cry for help score and an innocuous comment. Being overconfident about the direction to take is also a risk where stepping back and reflecting on alternatives provide the necessary pause.

Getting the balance right is not as easy as it seems. Leaders and managers attempting to do too much or too little with human capital metrics is a classic. You get over-inspired by the team discussion on what needs to change. You overestimate what can be done, and you overpromise on time and money ...

Overcoming limitations and obstacles

- Just as you would for market and customer decisions, wrap an analytical culture around your talent management decisions.
- Remember "analytical" includes "action-oriented" and switching between the two as appropriate. Do not get lost in the data. The end goal is action.
- Seek information and opinions from a variety of colleagues to widen your frame of reference and push your mind in fresh directions.
- How/when do you aim to achieve all the actions? Prioritize 1–3 actions.
- Reemphasize the importance of team ownership and accountability; action planned by the team is likely to be recognized by it as more effective.
- Challenge yourself and the team as to how you can best influence and measure change.
- Take a balanced approach, promise, evaluate, and do what is realistic, not too much or too little, or, over or under your capability— just spot on.

8

Metrics for Skeptics

During my career, I have come across many colleagues who have not only been skeptical about human capital metrics, but also bored with them. Admittedly, it is not the world's most exciting topic and without real care and attention it can be rather dull! I have even experienced one colleague with an analytical background from academia turning into a skeptic when joining a business organization in a HR manager role on the grounds that metrics apply to research, not in the real business world!

Human capital metrics are often made cumbersome and complex, perhaps also to wrap certain exclusivity around it. In the business context, metrics should be exactly the opposite of cumbersome and complex. The idea of "metrics for skeptics" was generously given to me by a former colleague and this chapter is devoted to the typical skeptics you may encounter and how to tackle and overcome their skepticism.

The kinds of skeptics you may encounter

In the following, we will meet a number of real-life skeptics—or archetypes of skepticism towards human capital metrics—and capture their worries and issues. We will look at what can be done to overcome their concerns and help move them away from being skeptics to having a healthier relationship to metrics and their use.

So, let us meet our skeptics:

- The CEO who already knows it all and primarily relies on his or her gut for people decisions. They have never been proven wrong in the past!
- The division or country leader who feels it does not apply here locally for cultural or other local reasons. Metrics are for head office. We do the business here.
- The busy manager who has a lot on his or her plate and often feels they are between a rock and a hard place when results are poor and puzzling. Now I know, what do I do about it?
- The new manager overwhelmed by it all. They have recently shifted from being in an expert contributor role where they were very well regarded for their contribution and now find they are overwhelmed by having to provide data and numbers all the while. If this is what leadership is all about, they are not sure they want to do it and would prefer to go back to being an individual contributor.
- The employee who provides feedback again and again and never sees any action or change happening, so why bother?
- The employee who is scared of numbers. He or she does not understand them, was never any good at math and is afraid of being found out.
- The process-driven HR professional who ticks the boxes for response rate, data coming in on time, or process compliance, but fails to frame and ground the purpose and content in the business as levers for development and change.
- The software-obsessed IT expert who questions usability and security of HR tools and technology and even hacks your systems to prove the point!
- The social-media mad communications expert who spends days and days and huge amounts of money chasing the magic metric amongst tons of dialogues and big data.
- The customer who just wants to buy and does not care to give feedback every time he or she has a brief interaction with your business.

Context for scenarios

All scenarios assume that the company already has a fairly well functioning human capital measurement and management framework in place. That is, you collect, distribute, and use as improvement targets for performance, a range of human capital metrics for teams and individual managers, such as diversity distribution, employee engagement, manager effectiveness, and performance rating. As discussed throughout this book, your human capital data collected and reported are related to business needs, reliable, open to scrutiny, accompanied by adequate explanation, presented in an easily understandable manner to the different target audiences, and enabling organization leaders and teams to identify appropriate improvement actions. In other words, your company is set up for success with good processes, tools, and content. Nevertheless, here come the skeptics.

The CEO who already knows it all

The CEO does not pay too much interest to human capital metrics. He does not feel the need to. He is mostly interested in top-line growth, sales numbers, and, when it comes to bottom-line management, financial metrics. His attitude is somewhat arrogant and he says things like "I can manage this company perfectly fine with the financial numbers I am used to and have done so for many years." "I am aware that people are a big part of our cost base and keep the people costs under control." "I spent more than 50% of my time visiting and talking to managers and employees. I know how they feel about working here." If you asked him directly, he would say that the people data he has seen has been biased, created unnecessary noise, and is difficult to take action on. People decisions on recruiting and developing managers and employees can just as well be made based on discussion, relationship, and gut feeling.

What to do about it

Talking the same language is always a good approach, so be ready with a convincing business case for how working with human capital metrics would make sense for your company. You may even introduce the idea of an analytical culture as a differentiator, what this involves, and how it is possible, as described in Chapter 1. Appeal to their vanity about the company being different from others and as such being able to position itself in the market both for talent and for sales in a different and more exciting way. Build a model and business case where you showcase how people data for the full talent management process or employee life cycle support better people decisions, differentiate your company, and emphasize people assets in addition to people costs.

Find a way of asking questions like: How does the way we look at people, asset-based or cost-based, impact our employer brand? Are people a part of our strategy? How do we become more of a people company? Employees talk together in and across companies and industries. They can, for example, check out glassdoor.com[1] for peer feedback and an inside view at jobs and companies before they make a decision to join or leave. The CEO's reputation is a big part of the employer brand. Old school has increasingly less appeal.

Most of the arguments and actions to bring the CEO round from his or her skepticism can be found in the introductory chapters of the book. Why do we bother about human capital metrics and working strategically with human capital metrics? In addition, you may want to do a People SWOT, summarizing your people strengths, weaknesses, opportunities, and threats and gather supporting data. A SWOT analysis[2] is normally used to provide a snapshot of the *entire* business position at a specific point in time and helps in the process of improving performance. The People SWOT would focus solely on employees. Strengths or weaknesses are internal aspects (things the company can control) and opportunities or threats are external aspects (things outside the control of the company). Strengths and opportunities are positive factors. Weaknesses and threats are negative factors.

Table 8.1   People SWOT to get stakeholder commitment to human capital metrics

People SWOT Example	Positives	Negatives
Internal factors	Strengths • Highly skilled workforce • Highly motivated workforce • Obsession with quality	Weaknesses • High staff turnover • Uneven productivity • Weak management • Poor innovation capability
External factors	Opportunities • Main competitor closing, take over best employees • Availability of skilled labor	Threats • Relocation of Headquarters due to new local legislation increasing costs • Poor Employer Brand

For each SWOT factor you would use people data to justify your findings and the People SWOT would, in fact, by itself prove the usability and applicability of human capital metrics (Table 8.1). A SWOT will appeal to senior leaders' vanity and help build an alliance amongst other senior leaders who can become allies.

It is also powerful to demonstrate the link between people data and business outcomes, e.g. motivated employees create extraordinary business results. As discussed earlier, work with the CFO to correlate human metrics with financial metrics. Invite in people the CEO admires and who are doing this. Find a way of identifying what the senior leaders are missing out on, e.g. that internal best practice is stronger for motivation and performance than external best practice!

The division or country leader who feels it does not apply here

Another skeptic is the division or country leader who is of the opinion that the specific division or country cannot be covered by generic human capital metrics. We are special, our talent is different, and our business culture is unique. We need a special process and if we are to use the common process, it needs to be altered to accommodate our special requirements. Until this happens, we cannot participate. This group of skeptics does not seem to challenge the premises of financial metrics, which are commonly used across borders and cultures. However, if human capital metrics should apply here, it needs to be altered and tailor-made to cater for special traits and unique differences. People decisions should be based and executed in the local context.

What to do about it

The first thing to do is to emphasize economies of scale. The company is using and applying the same set of human capital metrics in order to minimize cost and effort. It is also to avoid complexity and keep it simple.

Similarly, targets for key people data are set for and cascaded down into the full organization. All leaders are held accountable against the same set of human capital metrics (as with financial objectives) because it is the same overall strategy being executed. Benchmarks will include differences and biases inherent in division/function and country cultures and demographics and are hence representative for all divisions and leaders. Where it would make sense to use e.g. country benchmarks, such local yardsticks can be made available. There will, of course, be areas where only local people data would be applicable, for example, the pay and benefit area. This is the exception rather than the rule.

You are part of a whole. Wanting specific people data across the board is a symptom of silo thinking that may lead to an emotional disconnection from the rest of the company. It becomes "us" and "them," infighting and turf wars become frequent, and the organization is in danger of shifting from being externally focused to becoming internally focused and driven. In fact, when you use generic and global people data, this will soon direct you to the emotionally disconnected units and groups where company culture is less strong and talent not aligned and likely from my experience unhappy.

Many of the arguments and actions to alleviate the division or country leader's skepticism can be found in Chapters 3 and 4 of the book, the machine room of human capital metrics and determining what human capital metrics you need.

The busy manager

There is a lot on a manager's plate. Hectic and even stressful time periods are no doubt part of the job! The busy manager does not take the time to understand what the people data measures and what it means for his or her organization because he or she does not feel they have the time, they have conflicting priorities, and, more often than not, they do not see or feel the benefit. He or she may have trouble with numbers. He or she may lose the guiding link, email, or access details. There is all too much data and he or she feels completely overloaded. Where do you start and where do you end. They may be hesitant about what to do with the data. Great results may become an excuse to do nothing, not being able to identify anything to improve or change. Poor results may leave the manager feeling stalemate and not wanting to know.

What to do about it

Being realistic about the time it takes to be a manager is essential. People management represents XX% of the job (depending on your company and manager role). People measurement can actually make people management quicker and easier. You may want to invest the necessary time upfront to understand your human capital metrics. You take some time on your own to digest results. If measures are unclear or no or poor guidance provided, you may reach out to your HR manager for support. Another approach is discussing results with your manager or in your management team. Checking your perceptions with peers and making sense of results together makes things clearer. Finally, results should always be understood in the current business context. Is the division struggling to meet sales numbers? Has there just been a major reorganization? Factors outside the team must be taken into consideration.

Once you start following and using human capital metrics on a regular basis, you will remember where and how to access it. User names and passwords are annoying; however, most workplaces do not have single sign-on to tools and databases. If accessing is too cumbersome, it should be escalated to the IT department. It is worthwhile considering the possibility of single sign-on.

Dialogues with HR and IT on people data needed to execute the manager role effectively will help alleviate data overload. It is also important that corporate functions, often responsible for data collection and usage processes, talk together and align activities over the calendar year. For example, HR coordinates with CSR (Corporate Social Responsibility) and Finance to ensure that similar data are only collected once, that data is re-used as much as possible, and that results are reported in a coordinated manner to leaders and managers.

Moving from data to action is not easy. Again perceived lack of time and potential conflict with other organizational priorities are obstacles to overcome. Once you share results with the team or the individual, you will find that discussion brings life to the data and helps determine the key one or two issues upon which it will be most valuable to take action. You are likely to find inspiration and guidance on how to conduct sharing meetings/workshops and capture actions in your intranet or you can ask your HR manager for facilitation support.

Remember the basics. Keep it simple. Do not try to change everything. Just aim to do a couple of things really well. Be specific and target action upon issues you can easily influence. Outline what success will look like and when you expect it to be achieved. Assign responsibility for the action and encourage team involvement and individual accountability for change. This is not about the manager doing it all alone. Monitor progress. Revisit your action plan regularly and put it on your team meeting agenda once a month. Celebrate success and keep building momentum!

The good action you do personally or facilitate with others is guaranteed to drive your people data results upwards. Some good action is enough; it does not have to be plentiful and great. On the other hand, no action is likely to drive people data results downwards. In return for giving feedback and performance, employees expect improvement action and development for the better.

Some good action is enough; it does not have to be plentiful and great

The busy manager will find comfort in most chapters of this book, if only they can find the time to read it in full!

The overwhelmed new manager

> If there is a lot on an experienced manager's plate, the new manager probably feels even more pressure. New managers have often shifted from being an expert contributor where they were very well regarded for their contribution. Now they find themselves overwhelmed by having to look at and analyze data and numbers and communicate their response actions up and down the organization for the majority of their time. If this is what leadership is all about, they are not sure they want to do it and would prefer to go back to being an individual contributor. Some new managers have a tendency for micro-management, driven by the anxiety of being in a new job and a desire to

be successful, and this extends to many areas, including metrics. "There are rounding errors in this data set." "I need to find out who in my team gave what score, then I can query them about it."

What to do about it

I believe it is vital that people measurement and management are part of the training package offered to new managers. This will outline purpose, processes and tools, giving and receiving feedback, the feedback facilitator's role, calls to action for managers at different levels of the organization, etc. It is much easier to start out, as a manager, by using the available support process from the very beginning. There is really no value in postponing anything.

If new managers feel especially overwhelmed and lost in certain areas, they may reach out to more experienced managers—perhaps through their HR business partner—to be coached around these particular topics. Or they can discuss with the network of newly appointed managers. This will also be comforting as many new managers experience and need to tackle similar issues. If the organization does not have a network for newly appointed managers, I recommend that you establish one.

Good practice is to try to take the helicopter to get away from micromanagement. As a former expert, you will appreciate and be able to rely on the "experts" in the company, those in your own team and those in HR being responsible for people data and people processes. Try to refrain from wanting to know who said what when and instead use feedback proactively and with future improvement in mind.

You may also start out as a manager by developing a culture of measurement in your team and building your staff's ability to manage and use data. This may take some of the stress away from the manager. Delegation is one way of practicing leadership as opposed to micromanagement, and the team will feel involved and accountable. Your team members will be more ready to become managers at some point than you were!

Like the busy manager, the overwhelmed new manager will find help and guidance in most chapters of this book.

The employee who provides feedback again and again and never sees any action or change happening

You are an employee who is constantly being asked to provide feedback. Every time you switch on your laptop there seems to be another pop up screen on the intranet asking you to fill in a questionnaire. You have the feeling that you already filled in this questionnaire. Your manager keeps asking the team if you have answered to a survey. There are numerous reminder emails in your inbox. There is a competition in the division: the team with the highest response rate gets a reward! You provide your feedback, yet you do not recall seeing any communication on results or follow-up actions? People data depends on feedback from employees and employees are, therefore, entitled to get know the results and be part of changing things, not just filling in their feedback form. In approximately half of these feedback situations, employees do not get to understand or be involved in next steps such as team discussion, planning change action, and doing things differently.[3] This is not only frustrating, but diminishes the organization's appetite for development and capability to handle feedback. In my experience, this is especially frustrating for the younger generations at work who are used to and value real-time feedback, immediate action, constant change, and Internet speed.

What to do about it

A good starting point is to communicate broadly and consistently the organization's expectations and processes for feedback follow-up. Why are we concerned with this feedback? It is part of the organizational journey we are on at our company. Paying attention to what our employees are saying and using their feedback to drive change is important for today and tomorrow. The process is essentially one of understanding, sharing, and acting on results and findings, as described earlier. You may have variations of this basic process for different feedback scenarios. In any case, 80% effort is expected on feedback follow-up and 20% on feedback harvesting.

A focus on facilitation skills with managers and employees at large is essential. This can be in the form of training and/or guidance with tips and hints on feedback follow-up facilitation. What do you do as a facilitator? You ask people for their opinions and their interpretation. You record the issues as they are highlighted. You focus attention on the questions and issues the team can control and influence. You keep positive and focus on strengths as well as the opportunities for improvement. You use questions such as

What makes us successful as a team? What holds us back? What additional help do we need? What can we do together? What can I do?

You are now creating a feedback culture that is really quite desirable, as it unleashes employees' initiative, imagination, and passion—the things money cannot buy! Feedback is giving appropriate recognition, having frequent improvement discussion, and ongoing learning. Make it easy, social, and fun. It is an integral part of the work life. Everyone does it together. People actually want to do it.

Empathy is a competency inherent in a feedback culture. Empathy is walking a mile in another person's shoes. You will read the different generations at work more clearly and understand when a Gen Y team member asks for more feedback, it expresses a genuine desire to learn more. Feedback will help you promote retention; people will not leave due to insufficient recognition.

Empathy is walking a mile in another person's shoes

Finally, an audit of how much feedback is being requested in the whole company may be useful to get an overview, eliminate the non-essentials, and re-use data for different purposes.

The employee who is scared of numbers

There is the employee who is scared of numbers. He or she does not understand metrics, was never any good at math, and is afraid of being discovered. You diligently provide answers to surveys and the like, however, when it comes to reading and using metrics, you consciously try to avoid it. In team meetings and workshops, you keep silent, avoid asking questions and providing more input, because you do not want to expose your lack of skills and insecurity. This means the team and your company miss out on divergent thinking,[4] creativity and input from people who are more "right-brained" oriented, that is, more intuitive, thoughtful, and subjective, as opposed to "left-brained," that is, more logical, analytical, and objective.

What to do about it

Employees with a negative bias towards numbers may do well to take the training that is available around people data collection processes in the company. This will provide guidance on how to read, understand, and interpret the various types of metrics being applied. Training decks will typically be available for self-study on the intranet where also e-learning modules or recorded training sessions can be found.

Managers of employees who feel this way will hopefully detect their bias and encourage their employees to contribute towards a discussion around what the numbers tell us and how we can further address opportunities and weaknesses. Managers and facilitators will ensure that the quieter individuals speak up and come forward with their change ideas in groups and workshops.

The process-driven HR professional

Another skeptic I have often come across is the "compliance king or queen" kind of skeptic. It is a different form of skepticism. It stems from an inclination to be as efficient as possible and results in short-term focus and ignorance of longer-term organization benefits. The compliance king or queen is obsessed with the process, when what happens, who should do what, and what exactly HR should do. Ticking the boxes for compliance becomes the end goal, not building the organizational capabilities necessary to be able to adapt to changing customer demands and competing effectively.

What to do about it

While compliance is a good thing, it should not be the only focus. Too much compliance may make processes bureaucratic, complex, and slow. It also stands in the way of curiosity, initiative, and perspective. You may miss out on both the hard and the soft stuff. With little curiosity, you may not ask all the why questions for people data that will guide you to those counterintuitive nuggets that are really useful for promoting change. With limited initiative, you will never put people firmly on the agenda. With limited perspective, you may not hear and be able to act on rumors and corridor conversations. Missing out on hard and soft stuff inhibits your ability to sense what will happen next and get involved. The compliance king or queen also tends to believe that sorting out organizational ills is a task for leaders and managers, not HR. Toning down compliance may be what is necessary to be more involved, connected, and responsible within the business.

In recent research, Deloitte, a global consulting company, found that only 25% of business leaders believe their HR teams deliver excellent or good capabilities, compared to 75% who say HR is just getting by or underperforming.[5] To be an effective business partner, HR teams need an increasingly wide range of skills. Deloitte brands the HR professionals of the future as skilled business consultants. This would involve getting out the comfort zone of compliance and the prison of process obsession.

The software-obsessed IT expert

> The software-obsessed expert will question the tools and technology behind human capital metrics. Is the chosen cloud-based solution secure enough? Are people data well protected and individual responses kept confidential at all times? He or she may go to great lengths to try to hack your systems to prove non user-friendly functionality or inadequate data security. If you are a technology-based company, it may be difficult to protect your human capital systems against internal hackers who are both persistent and best in class. The buzz around human capital metrics will soon center on complaints about the tools not working properly and this can become quite distracting for everyone. You have to prove (one more time) that you invested in the best tool on the market and it does serve its purpose well.

What to do about it

Once the complaints reach the head of HR, you will have to defend the tools and technology investment. You should be confident about your choice if it is based on a business case, market scan, and vendor screening. You may then want to express a little frustration with colleagues who are supposed to be spending their time on developing the company's software, not hacking HR tools and technology.

Ideally, you will work with your software-obsessed experts, gather their feedback and hand this over to your external vendor. Next, you will want to ensure that proper change requests are part of the vendor's roadmap. This dialogue will also help to gradually bring your internal hackers over on your side and they now focus on how human capital measurement supports managing the business.

Complaints about tools can become a displacement activity. Employees may deflect their concerns about poor results onto tool problems. Tool problems are not personal and can be addressed more easily. Your challenge is to get attention back to what the human capital metrics are telling us so that you can start to facilitate common understanding and targeted action.

The social-media mad communications expert chasing the magic metric

The "social-media mad communications expert" is never really happy about any particular human capital metric. It is never quite right and we keep chasing the magic metric that will tell us the ultimate truth. This skeptic is obsessed with collaboration and crowd sourcing, generating a mass of data, but often has no sense of how to analyze and apply it. They want everything to be public, transparent, and available, resulting in the process becoming over engaging, over complicated, and without focus on change. In the end, we brand it right so that it fits into the story we would like to tell and want to believe in.

What to do about it

While it is great to want to have perfect and proprietary metrics, ambition can be unrealistic and chasing that magic metric becomes an end in itself. It is no longer about how you can use and apply people data in the business. Employees are confused by all the social media initiatives such as blogs, online communities, polls, and surveys, sponsored by leadership and communications. Social-media madness, some would claim. Leadership teams and HR try to make sense of ratings and statistics, which will often show that, after the initial excitement, activity levels drop like a stone. The social-media strategy should be aligned with the must-win battles and kept simple in order for people inputs and metrics to support execution of business priorities. As previously noted, data never changes anything. Could we count on the magic metric? In fact, we are not after the truth but those people interventions that will sustain our company's success.

Story telling around data is powerful. What is this data really telling us? Is there an overarching theme? What topics appear when we compare quantitative and qualitative data? How are perceptions across cultures and generations in the workplace? It should, however, be a true-to-the-data story, not a story that senior leaders or stakeholders would like to hear. I have often witnessed that results and findings become "branded." You almost know the outcome from the beginning, this data will be part of that story. Employees see through branding immediately, this is not our reality, and hard earned trust may be gone in a snap.

The customer who just wants to buy

Even though customer measures are peripheral in this book, they can be used to compare employee perceptions against. So the customer deserves a little space here, too. Customers come online (phone or web) or into your shop to browse and buy. Today, it seems, even the briefest of encounters triggers a customer feedback request. You call your bank to renew a deposit agreement. The actual call takes five minutes (after having corresponded with a machine voice and waited on the line for the agent). This is very little interaction to form an opinion on. Customers may wonder how they can rate their experience and end up giving high scores because they are nice people. The bank continues with this fragile feedback routine as good scores boost rewards.

What to do about it

The same criteria would apply for customer metrics as for human capital metrics—they should be relevant, reliable, and actionable. A customer just wanting to buy will no doubt deem these basic criteria unfulfilled in many feedback situations.

Using empathy when designing customer feedback loops may be useful. This will help looking at it from the customer's point-of-view. What is critical about the customer experience? How will we use the feedback to improve the customer experience? How frequent do we need to source feedback? Using analytics when making sense of customer feedback may distinguish customer loyalty. One day, that silly feedback request may make you change your buying habits and you will go shopping somewhere else.

9

Calls to Action

I would like to end this book as I began it, however, at this point without the "if." We now assume that in business we do aspire to make more evidence driven people decisions and take more targeted people actions and, therefore, we must bother about human capital metrics. We can remove the "if."

People are a valuable asset, as they amount to a minimum of 30% of the cost base of a company. Using metrics to continuously improve and innovate the way we work, collaborate, and compete is bound to impact the business bottom-line. People unlike machines cannot be turned on and off at random but must sit in fitting roles and be motivated to contribute with passion, creativity, and that extraordinary performance when they are at work. Human capital metrics provide a dialogue platform where all teams, leaders, and employees share and act on feedback about important aspects of the company and workplace.

As mentioned in Chapter 1, we can boil the ingredients of an agile and healthy performance culture down to:

1. A work environment that is both externally and internally focused.
2. Teams where diversity, collaboration, and execution are characteristics.
3. Leadership on purpose from the boardroom to the front lines.

This is the kind of caring and buzzing work environment you want in your company. You know it when you see it, but people data helps you to monitor and evolve it.

So, the question is, what now? There could be these calls to action for the five different scenarios below, depending on where you are with your metrics:

- The scenario where your company does not work with human capital metrics, but would like to start. A place to start is with employee engagement using the manual in Chapter 6.
- The scenario where your company does work with human capital metrics and you want to take it further. A way of reviewing and evolving your approach is comparing with the toolbox as described in Chapter 5.
- For both of the above scenarios, you can run an innovative process to harvest ideas for application and adaptation.
- Whatever road you follow, please remember to take the prescribed medicine. The end goal should be change for the better.
- Down the road, leaders and teams will start asking questions like "What do the best leaders at our company do?" and "What characterizes high-performing teams here?" This is when you want to document and replicate internal best practice.

Your company starts with measurement

This is the scenario where your company does not work with human capital metrics, but would like to start. A place to start is with employee engagement, as this will give you broad feedback on how it is to work here, how your teams collaborate and perform, the quality of leaders and senior management, degree of customer focus, your company culture, and how committed employees are with respect to giving their discretionary effort and wanting to stay with the organization.

Engagement is important because it is about purpose. Why do we work and how can we develop? Measuring engagement helps to ensure that a high performance culture is healthy, human, and grounded in the company's values. Getting experience with this important process as a start is excellent on boarding to working with metrics in general, both as feedback and as a basis for decision-making and action.

You can use Chapter 6 as a script for all stages, from building the business case and elevator pitch, as well as other communications, for employee engagement inside the organization, through developing the survey questionnaire and assigning accountabilities, to survey follow-up, taking appropriate actions on the measures, and monitoring progress.

The survey process functions as a dialogue platform where all teams and employees share and act on feedback about important aspects of the company and workplace. Survey follow-up unleashes excitement and focus around improving and innovating the way we work, collaborate, and compete. In Chapter 6, there are a number of frameworks and templates to support the survey process becoming a dialogue platform and survey follow-up being involving and relevant:

- Template with CEO/CXO quotes to show senior management's commitment to employee engagement (Figure 6.1)
- Matrix showing the interplay of engagement and performance where you want to aim for high engagement AND high performance as in the top right-hand box (Table 6.2)
- Accountability matrix with roles and responsibilities for employee engagement in the full organization (Table 6.3)
- Framework for employee engagement research and survey supplier screening (Table 6.4)
- Template for two-layered survey follow-up process for organization and team (Table 6.5)
- Example of survey measures in your employee engagement survey (Figure 6.2)
- Agenda template for 60-minute team workshop for sharing results and agreeing action areas (Table 6.6)
- Template for capturing and committing to strengths, changes, and actions in groups/by individuals (Figure 6.3)

- Heat map identifying priorities for action planning (Figure 6.4)
- Gap closure method for setting and monitoring improvement targets (Table 6.7).

These frameworks and templates are easy to use within your contextual setting. As T.S. Eliot said: "Minor poets loan, major poets steal." To build the business case, you can also use Chapters 1 and 2, and, if you want to include a People SWOT analysis, you can use the guidance in Chapter 8 in connection with the CEO as a metrics skeptic.

Your company evolves measurement and management

This is the scenario where your company already uses and applies people data. A way of reviewing and evolving your approach is comparing with the metrics toolbox for managers as described in Chapter 5. Do your metrics cover the full Employee Life Cycle and key talent decisions that managers make over a workday, month, and year? How actionable are your current metrics? Do they help you drive the changes necessary to improve your business? Are the different stakeholders motivated to understand, share, and act on your people data? How well does your current approach create a culture of metrics? What gets in the way? What works well?

This would involve doing a little audit of what metrics you have in place for what stakeholder groups: HR, senior management, and managers. For example, whether we have enough metrics to support leaders and managers with their daily tasks, whether we have enough metrics to incentivize employees to develop and change, or whether we have enough leading metrics to make us sufficiently agile.

A further check concerns how well your current metrics hold stakeholders accountable for talent management. For example, what is in it for employees? Are employees excited to give and receive feedback and do they take ownership of their own development and team/organization improvement actions?

what is in it for employees?

Perhaps you will find that your metrics are in order and all you need to do is a re-launch and re-positioning! You explain the why again, providing a clear vision of what you want to accomplish, not compliance, but a compass for change. You update the training you conduct on processes and tools as well as on competences and skills such as feedback facilitation and change management. If you do not have training, you can develop it.

Inspiration on how to evolve measurement and management can also be found in Chapters 3 and 4, for example, combining quantitative and qualitative data, the organization's approach to sharing human capital metrics, applying supply chain thinking, and exploring real-time and proprietary "baseball" metrics.

Running an innovation process to boost application

In my experience, the easier part is setting up the measurement framework and the more difficult part is getting the people data to work across the organization and with all stakeholders. With respect to application, adaptation, and accountability, there is room for improvement and one call to action is—at regular intervals—to run an innovative process around how we apply and hold ourselves accountable for people data.

In Chapter 3, I used the following three company values, "delighting customers," "being passionate about innovation," and "respecting the individual," to illustrate a qualitative input metric type. I also talked about a quantitative measure for adaptation of company values in Chapter 6. In the employee engagement survey you would typically have a statement such as "At this company we live and breathe our values" which is asked to your entire employee population and you will see ratings by manager, team, function, division, country, and so forth.

An innovative process can be conducted to enhance the application, adaptation, and accountability of metrics in your company. This involves:

- Generating ideas
- Sorting ideas
- Processing ideas for implementation.[1]

Your focus area is the company values. Senior management would like the company values to be known and lived in every corner of the company. One focus question is: How can each of us live the values at work every day? The innovative process is shown in Table 9.1 with inputs and outputs per process stage.

The innovative process as outlined in Table 9.1 provides you with prioritized ideas ready for implementation for the focus question: How

Table 9.1   Innovative process for application, adaptation and accountability of people data

Innovative Process Stage	Input	Output
Generating ideas: playful, intuitive, open, creative	• Brainstorming: generate as many ideas as possible based on the focus area. • Association Technique: Make a chain of 20 random words (holiday, flower, grandmother …). Get ideas by taking each word and associating it with the focus question.	• Post-It notes with ideas
Sorting ideas: analytical, systematic, thorough	• Idea Sieve: as a group agree on 2–3 selection criteria. Each individual rates the criteria on the 1–5 scale. Ideas are sorted accordingly. • Traffic Lights: green ideas go through, yellow ideas are put on hold, and red ideas are discarded.	• Ideas bank with evaluated ideas
Processing ideas for implementation: solution-oriented enterprising, bold, pragmatic	• Idea Baton: the individual writes down a priority idea and a description of it. This description is passed like a baton to 8–10 peers who write down their improvement ideas on what can make the idea better, thinking bold and big! • Value Wheel: the group discusses and documents. Who, how and why will this idea delight and create value? Easy/hard to implement?	• Detailed description of all prioritized ideas • Value Wheel • SWOT (as described in Chapter 8)

can each of us live the values at work every day? A further output from the process is the idea bank of additional suggestions, which can be developed and implemented in due course. Here are some real-life examples of prioritized ideas:

- Have a value day at each site ending with a party.
- Appoint value champions for dedicated values in different functions, e.g. for "delighting customers" in sales, "being passionate about innovation" in R&D, and "respecting the individual" in the senior management team.

The process can be conducted for the whole company, a unit/function, or individual teams, depending on where your metrics indicate there is a need. It is important that the focus area and focus questions concern the management part, not the measurement framework. This is about each stakeholder using data to drive change, feeling involved, and being held accountable for high performance.

Taking the prescribed medicine

Data never changes anything by itself, but must be accompanied by action. As in medicine, diagnostics is good, but it is the treatment that makes you better. In Chapters 7 and 8, we have looked at reasons why taking the prescribed cure is sometimes difficult in the corporate setting and what can be done to swallow the pill.

Whether you start with measurement or evolve measurement and management, constantly check that your metrics are actionable both in the current business context and in the strategic setting. This is about actively shaping the game, not just playing the game you find. The end goal should be change.

check that your metrics are actionable both in the current business context and in the strategic setting

With the toolbox for managers in Chapter 5 you have 11 "standard" tools available. When you use those tools well, you construct a diverse team, build and sustain high performance, put the right people in the right room to execute your strategy, and develop yourself as a leader. I trust you will be able to pick the tools that are appropriate in the situation, also depending on your manager level and scope of leadership responsibilities.

If we look at career path ratios, it is clear that this metric is used differently in different scenarios. To recap, the Career Path Ratio measures total promotions relative to total transfers, with promotion being an upward movement in the organization and transfer being a lateral movement. As an organization grows, there are lots of promotion opportunities. As organization growth slows down, the number of promotions to lateral moves may significantly reduce. At this point, a big percentage (depending on growth and slump rates, but let us say 50%) of the employees will never be promoted or moved to a higher job grade again in their careers. The company and its managers will have to change course of action. The notion of career becomes focused on lateral moves, the employee value proposition, professional development expectations, and compensation. Career path ratio is still a meaningful and actionable metric; however, benchmarking and application change in the new business reality.

When the tools are used to build a strong house, it will get noted outside. You also build your brand as a trustworthy employer.

Replicating internal best practice

At some point leaders and teams will start asking questions like "What do the best leaders at our company do?" and "What characterizes high-performing teams here?" This is when you want to document and replicate internal best practice.

You have plenty of metrics to make a screening of teams and their leaders. Examples are the Manager Effectiveness Index and Employee Engagement Index from the toolbox as described in Chapter 5. You select your measure and rank all teams, highest index score to lowest index score. You then choose teams in the top quartile segment who also represent key talent for the business and demonstrate high performance in terms of profit, customer satisfaction, or quality. The leader and a couple of team members from each team are interviewed and the competences, behaviors, and ways of working characteristic of the teams documented. Now you have your internal best practice articulated and it can be celebrated, shared, and replicated.

I once captured such internal best practice in a small guide that I complied for a company where I previously worked. I called it *Great Managers, Great Teams* and for years it was the most downloaded document from the company's HR intranet site. Impressively, those great teams manage to overcome issues that might ordinarily be considered challenging when creating a truly engaging team culture: gender diversity, a diverse range of nationalities, geographical distribution across multiple countries and time zones, large team sizes, and a mix a contractor and permanent staff. Great managers display the ten competencies, behaviors, and ways of working as shown in Table 9.2.

Table 9.2   Internal Best Practice—competences, behaviors, and ways of working as displayed by engaged managers and engaged teams in one company

Great Managers	Create Great Teams
1. Are great communicators	• Meet regularly with their teams, virtually, e.g. bi-weekly calls, and face-to-face every six months at a minimum. Use transparent communications, e.g. wikis, blogs, Halo sessions, face-to-face time. Is approachable with an open door. • Cascade news on business strategy, objectives, and organizational changes quickly to help ensure their team is best placed and aligned to support the company going forward. • Promote two-way communication: encouraging all employees to contribute honestly in discussions, addressing questions and concerns promptly, and make themselves fully available to staff. • Follow up on employee engagement results. Make follow-up a team mandate. Delegate action planning. Monitor progress at team meetings.

(continued)

Continued

Great Managers	Create Great Teams
2. Know their teams	• Make an effort to understand how the team operates as a whole (using tools such as TMS[2] team types) and as individuals: learning styles, developmental needs and ambitions of each team member.
3. Know their customers	• Actively seek and use feedback from customers, particularly direct customers, and structure the work to promote as much interaction as possible between their teams and the business.
4. Know their competition	• Keep themselves and their team informed through team meetings, regular blog postings, store visits.
5. Know where they are going	• Know the objectives of the company. Understand how they contribute to the bigger picture. Have a clear and definite plan of how to get there. Dedicate time to discuss this with the team.
6. Challenge their teams	• Address poor performance promptly, objectively, and always in a confidential one-to-one setting. • Team members are regularly encouraged to share their learning objectives and progress with the rest of the team. • Encourage development and explore opportunities within and outside their division such as taking the lead on specialist projects and sharing knowledge inside and outside the team. • Coach individuals and apply reverse coaching.
7. Recognize staff appropriately	• Provide recognition where it is due through verbal, informal structures such as "Recognizing You" awards, and formal processes such as the performance management process. • Use praise a lot, in the open, and by the individual, depending on the preferred way. • Promoting team success by encouraging team members to publicly credit others for their contributions.
8. Know how to network	• Use their contacts in the business to promote their staff and facilitate their learning, e.g. inviting business leaders to share strategy. • Get support from HR to communicate employee engagement results and facilitate action planning. • Delegate external and internal speaking opportunities to staff. • Use all available tools to best effect.

(continued)

Continued

Great Managers	Create Great Teams
9. Lead by example, creating an inclusive, respectful and "can do" culture	• **Mutual respect**: by trusting and empowering employees to take decisions, delegating effectively, getting hands-on with the work itself when required, being supportive and expecting others to act the same. • **Inclusion**: promoting diversity, no hierarchy, not having favorites nor tolerating politics. • **Well-being**: showing consideration of time zones in scheduling meetings, maintaining work-life balance for themselves, encouraging time in lieu for overtime. • **Celebrating success**: publicly acknowledging excellent individual performance and having corporate celebrations such as "champagne toasts" to mark team successes. Helping others where required and asking for help when needed.
10. Are not afraid to be human	• Are respected and build relationships with the team members first as colleagues and second as direct reports. • Facilitate opportunities and activities around getting to know colleagues on a personal as well as a professional level.

When managers work like this, their teams also work like this. Managers become role models. There is a ripple effect and it becomes a virtuous circle.

Internal best practice is hugely motivating because people will recognize it as "ours." It is part of our culture and if that team over there can do it, so can we. It is aspirational and achievable. The thing is every company has to find internal best practice for itself. However, this call to action, I can guarantee, pays off quickly and plentifully.

Internal best practice is hugely motivating because people will recognize it as "ours"

Appendix 1: Alphabetical List of Human Capital Metrics

Human Capital Metric	Calculation	Usage	High/Low (direction-giving and dependent on e.g. industry)
Average Annual Salary per Full-Time Employee	Total annual salary/ full-time employees	A measure showing average base pay relative to full-time employees. You use the Average Annual Salary per Employee to manage your salary costs, which most probably constitute a major expense. You benchmark for compliance with company pay philosophy and employee expectations.	Targets related to compensation are influenced by many factors. You may set relative targets based on how you want to differ from talent competition. If you aim to provide higher salary levels to attract and retain talent, you want to target to be in the 75th percentile (top 25%) of industry competition. If you aim to be in low-cost locations, you target to be in the median.
Career Path Ratio	Total promotions/ total transfers	A metric showing the relation between upwards movement and lateral movement. Remember the pyramid-shaped or hierarchical organization has limited promotion	A ratio close to 1 probably means your company, division, or team is practicing too many promotions and too few transfers.

(continued)

Continued

Human Capital Metric	Calculation	Usage	High/Low (direction-giving and dependent on e.g. industry)
		capacity, however, almost unlimited transfer capacity.	
Diversity Distribution	End of period headcount by diversity dimension/ end of period headcount × 100	Diversity Distribution shows a breakdown of relevant diversity dimensions. Diversity Distribution metrics could include: age, gender, function, nationality, position, and/or tenure/life stage.	Ideally, your diversity distribution matches the marketplace in which you compete. As the marketplace is becoming more and more global, diversity is also more important.
Employee Engagement Index	Average of % favorable scores of question items in the index	High levels of employee engagement predict employees' willingness to go above and beyond and their intent to stay with the organization. Low levels of employee engagement indicate organization barriers to high performance and talent retention.	A rule of thumb: high is more than 70% favorable on the index; low is less than 70% favorable on the index. Or it is relative to a benchmark: High +5% Low −5%.
Employee Photos	N/A	Qualitative input in the form of employee-produced photos may help to create relevance for the individual employee and connect organizations and individuals.	High: more than 40% of population produce photos Low: less than 20% of population giving input.

(continued)

Continued

Human Capital Metric	Calculation	Usage	High/Low (direction-giving and dependent on e.g. industry)
Free Text Comments	N/A	Qualitative data in the form of free text comments make employees feel that they are listened to and their opinions count in developing the organization.	High: more than 40% of population give free text comments Low: less than 20% of population giving input.
Job Heat Map	A heat map is a composition type of metric where you break down your team or division into parts while allocating the level of significance or differentiation to each part. Processes and jobs are defined and shown as core, competitive, and differentiating	This measure is a way of segmenting the jobs within your team or division and pointing attention to those jobs that make a clear and positive difference in your ability to succeed in the marketplace. A heat map may kick-start discussion about performance variation and what it means for your teams.	High/low will depend on the scenario at hand: What and where are my core, competitive, and differentiating roles? How do the existing people I have in the roles perform? What development is needed? Where do I focus my attention?
Manager Effectiveness Index	Average of % favorable scores of question items in the index	An index metric showing how subordinates rate managers. The Manager Quality Index typically reflects the company's desired leadership competencies.	High: more than 70% favorable on the index Low: less than 70% favorable on the index. Or relative to a benchmark: High +5% Low –5%.

(continued)

Continued

Human Capital Metric	Calculation	Usage	High/Low (direction-giving and dependent on e.g. industry)
New Hire % of High Performers	Newly hired employees with high performance rating/all high performers × 100	A metric showing how many newly hired employees become high performers in per cent of all high performers.	High: more than 15% or new hire high performer % segment more than all high performer % segment Low: less than 10% or lower than new hires' proportion of average headcount.
Offer Acceptance Rate	Accepted offers/ extended offers × 100	A measure indicating the effectiveness of your recruiting process, value of employer brand, and offer strength.	High: more than 90% Low: less than 70%. Or relative to a benchmark. High >75th percentile.
Operating Profit per Employee	Operating profit/ full-time employees	A measure showing operating profit relative to full-time employees.	You may want to target to be in the 75th percentile (top 25%) of a relevant benchmark group, for example your industry, as higher profits per employee in most cases equates to higher productivity.
Rehire Rate	Rehires/total external hires × 100	A metric showing how many former employees the company recruits back.	A target could be to have 10% of new hires sourced from former employees.
Survey Follow-Up	Average of % favorable scores of question items in the index	Measurement of behavioral change. Would cover team leaders and senior management, e.g. My team/Senior management has taken action based on feedback from the last survey.	High: more than 60% favorable on the index. Low: less than 40% favorable on the index.

(*continued*)

Continued

Human Capital Metric	Calculation	Usage	High/Low (direction-giving and dependent on e.g. industry)
Tenure Distribution	End of period headcount by tenure type/ end of period headcount × 100	Tenure distribution shows how many employees you have in each tenure group.	Ideally, the total workforce tenure composition matches the marketplace in which you compete with employees thinking and acting like your customers.
Termination Reason Breakdown	Termination by termination reason/all terminations × 100	A breakdown of all terminations into termination reasons showing the number and/ or percentage allocated to each termination reason.	Make sure to have a fit-for-purpose termination breakdown (type and reason) to track relevant factors and be able take targeted actions.
Top Talent Recommendation	Strongly agree + agree responses by top talent/all responses by top talent × 100	An index metric indicating the degree to which top talent (as defined by your company) would recommend your company as a great place to work.	High: top talent scores higher than average. Low: top talent scores lower than average. Or target interval of +/–90% favorable.
Training Hours per Employee	Total training hours/ full-time employees	A measure indicating the average time an employee spends on formal learning and development activities.	High: more than 80 hours per employee. Low: less than 8 hours. Targets can be detailed for general competencies (customer service, leadership) or technical competencies.
Turnover Rate	Terminated employees/ average headcount × 100	A metric showing the percentage of leavers out of your average headcount. It is useful to	High: more than 20%. Low: less than 5%.

(continued)

Continued

Human Capital Metric	Calculation	Usage	High/Low (direction-giving and dependent on e.g. industry)
		distinguish between voluntary and involuntary leavers. You may also want other breakdowns of this metric, for example high performer turnover rate.	
Turnover Rate High Performers	Total number of high-performing employees that terminated in a given period/the average high performer population in your team/ division over the same period × 100	The level of high performers leaving will point to factors around what your company offers, both in terms of extrinsic drivers such as rewards and benefits, but probably more in terms of intrinsic drivers. Is your team a hot spot to be? Combined with the Termination Reason Breakdown, what can you do to stop high performers from leaving?	How do you measure up to company internal turnover rates for high performers? Also, how is your turnover rate high performers compared to overall turnover rate? A high performer turnover greater than overall turnover means you bleed talent.

Appendix 2: List of Illustrations

Found in Chapter	Figure number and name	Is an illustration of
1. Why Bother about Human Capital Metrics?	**Box 1.1**: Elements and characteristics of an analytical culture	What an analytical culture contains, organization competencies of agility, transparency, and consensus and related behaviors. Can be used as a benchmark.
2. Working Strategically with Human Capital	**Table 2.1**: Maturity matrix where organization maturity drives usage and application of human capital metrics	How strategic usage and application depend on organization maturity. Characteristics of level 1, 2, and 3 organizations and impact on application of human capital metrics. Can be used to target ambition level and implementation desire.
3. The Machine Room	**Table 3.1**: Overview of metric types and examples of each metric type	Understanding metric types is a prerequisite for identifying metrics for measurement needs and for interpreting measurements. Two examples of each metric type are subsequently outlined and detailed.
	Table 3.2: Termination type and reason breakdown	Provides an example of how this measure is calculated and can be used when broken down into real-life termination types and termination reasons.
	Table 3.3: Examples of SMART (Specific, Measurable, Achievable, Realistic, and Time-bound) versus DUMB (Dull, Unclear, Mundane, and Boring) targets	Provides examples of SMART and DUMB target setting for two specific targets: (1) Reduction in high performers leaving the company and (2) Increase in managers' participation in internal blogging.

(continued)

Continued

Found in Chapter	Figure number and name	Is an illustration of
4. Determining What Measures You Need	**Table 4.1**: Using the Employee Life Cycle to determine what metrics you need. The ten metric examples are from Chapter 3	Is used to ensure that your chosen metrics cover all talent decisions within the Employee Life Cycle from recruiting through engaging, developing, leading, managing, and rewarding to exiting talent.
	Figure 4.1: Applying supply-chain thinking to detailing people decisions and metric requirements	Can be used to link for example recruiting and on boarding processes, activities and decision points to a supply chain of talent in order to determine what human capital metrics are most impactful.
	Figure 4.2: Using the Johari Window to identify metrics that will illuminate hidden characteristics, blind spots and unknown potential	Is applied when thinking broadly and boldly about what human capital metrics to work with.
	Table 4.2: Actions and metrics/targets to satisfy employee engagement drivers	How you take your key drivers of employee engagement and turn them into actions at the same time allocating human capital metrics to monitor progress on actions.
5. A Toolbox for Managers	**Figure 5.1**: Data value curve and how different data builds evidence driven and analytical capacity in the organization	Provides an overview of data sources, how the HRIS (Human Resource Information System) constitute the foundation and how data value is built from relative checks to being able to make predictions.
	Table 5.1: The eleven human capital metrics covering the Employee Life Cycle included in the toolbox	Provides an overview of the 11 basic metrics in the toolbox for managers and which part of the talent management process they belong to.
	Figure 5.2: Heat map showing organization processes and jobs that are most differentiating	Provides an example of how to group jobs by criticality to understand what core, competitive, and differentiating roles you have and where they are.

(continued)

Continued

Found in Chapter	Figure number and name	Is an illustration of
6. Making It Happen	**Table 6.1**: The post-data process where you manage your human capital	Getting an overview of activities in the post-data process, which is where 80% of your effort should be allocated!
	Figure 6.1: CEO/ CXO quotes to show senior management's commitment to employee engagement	A tip is to showcase top management's commitment by collecting and communicating personal stories or quotes from the CEO (or fellow leaders) as part of the reasons why employee engagement makes a difference at your company.
	Table 6.2: Interplay of engagement and performance where you want to aim for high engagement AND high performance as in the top right-hand box	Characteristics of organizations with combinations of high/ low engagement and high/low performance. Where are you?
	Table 6.3: Accountability matrix with roles and responsibilities for employee engagement in the full organization	Can be used to assign accountability in the organization to employees, line managers, functional leaders, senior management, and HR for their part in creating an awesome place to work.
	Table 6.4: Framework for employee engagement research and survey supplier screening	An example of Request for Proposal areas against which different suppliers can be rated in order to invite for beauty parades or final selection.
	Table 6.5: Two-layered survey follow-up process	The two-layered survey follow-up process is used to tailor results reporting, calls to action, and improvement targets to organization level (for leadership teams) and team level (for managers).
	Figure 6.2: Example of survey measures in your employee engagement survey	Can be used as a checklist for themes to be included in an employee engagement process.
	Table 6.6: Agenda for 60-minute team workshop for sharing results and agreeing action areas	This example agenda is used to conduct the results sharing and action-planning workshop with teams. 60 minutes is the minimum time you should spend.

(continued)

Continued

Found in Chapter	Figure number and name	Is an illustration of
	Figure 6.3: Template for capturing and committing to strengths, changes, and actions in groups/by individuals	Using a template to capture what we already have (our strengths), what we could do better (our changes), and how each of us can support the changes (our actions) serves several purposes.
	Figure 6.4: Heat map identifying priorities for action planning	Heat map with quadrants (keep on doing, build on this strength, watch this, act immediately) for what action areas belong where and how urgently actions need to be established.
	Table 6.7: Gap-closure method for setting improvement targets	Applying the gap closure method for setting improvement targets for people data. The gap closure method is a fair way of setting improvement targets as it takes into account where you currently are relative to a benchmark.
8. Metrics for Skeptics	**Table 8.1**: People SWOT to get stakeholder commitment to human capital metrics	Provides a filled example of a People SWOT (Strengths, Weaknesses, Opportunities, and Threats) to be used to as part of the business case for using and applying human capital metrics in your company.
9. Calls to Action	**Table 9.1**: Innovative process for application, adaptation and accountability of people data	Can be used to boost and improve how metrics are used and applied across the organization and with stakeholders. The innovative process involves idea generation, idea selection, and processing ideas for implementation.
	Table 9.2: Internal Best Practice—competences, behaviors, and ways of working as displayed by engaged managers and engaged teams in one company	Illustrates how to describe and document internal best practice in terms of engaging leadership and engaged teams. Once captured, internal best practice can be shared and replicated.

Notes

1: Why Bother about Human Capital Metrics?

1. www.oxforddictionaries.com/definition/english/human-capital (2014).
2. C. Rosenthal (2013), *Plantations Practiced Modern Management. Harvard Business Review*, Harvard Business Publishing, Watertown, MA.
3. Attributed to Peter Drucker (2006) in relation with management consultancy to Ford Motor Company (the exact quote cannot be sourced. Peter Drucker was an Austrian-born American management consultant).
4. www.edelman.com (2014).
5. Gallup, Kenexa/IBM, Towers Watson and Hay Group are examples.
6. Accenture (2008), Newsroom: Most U.S. Companies Say Business Analytics Still Future Goal, Not Present Reality. Available at: http://newsroom.accenture.com/article_display.cfm?article_id=4777.
7. Deloitte Consulting (2014), Global Human Capital Trends. Available at: http://www2.deloitte.com/global/en/pages/human-capital/articles/human-capital-trends-2014.html.

2: Working Strategically with Human Capital

1. Porter, M. (1996), *What Is Strategy? Harvard Business Review*, Harvard Business Publishing, Watertown, MA.
2. IBM (2014), IBM software, Information Management. Available at: http://www-01.ibm.com/software/data/quality/.
3. Horngren (2013), *Cost Accounting*, Pearson, London.
4. *McKinsey Quarterly* (1997), *The War for Talent* (2001), McKinsey & Company, New York.

3: The Machine Room

1. E.g. Cascio, W., Boudreau, J. (2011), *Investing in People*, New Jersey: Pearson Education and Davenport; T. H., Harris, J. G, Morison, R. (2010), *Analytics at Work*, Mass: Harvard Business School.
2. Meredith, K., Sanford, S., Proctor, B., and Freire, P. (2005), *The Metrics Standard*, Establishing Standards for 200 Core Human Capital Metrics, Corporate Leadership Council. Washington, US, London, UK.
3. Human Capital Management Institute (2013), *Human Capital Metrics Handbook*.
4. The LEGO Group, Annual Report 2013. Annual reports can be found at http://www.lego.com/da-dk/aboutus/lego-group/annual-report.
5. Sullivan, Dr. John (2013), *Leading Edge Talent Management*. Available at http://www.slideshare.net/drjohnsullivan/leading-edge-talent-management.
6. Gratton, L. (2014), *Future of Work*, www.lyndagratton.com
7. www.fortune.com (2014).
8. www.reputationinstitute.com (2014).

4: Determining What Measures You Need

1. Huselid, M., Becker, B., and Beatty, R. (2005), *The Workforce Scorecard*. Boston, Massachusetts: Harvard Business School Press.
2. Cascio, W. and Boudreau, J. (2011), *Investing in People: Financial Impact of Human Resource Initiatives*. New Jersey: Pearson Education.
3. The two metrics are part of the 200 core human capital measures in the earlier referenced Metrics Standard by the Corporate Leadership Council and InfoHRM (2005).
4. Luft, J. and Ingham, H. (1955). "The Johari window, a graphic model of interpersonal awareness." *Proceedings of the Western Training Laboratory in Group Development*, Los Angeles: UCLA.
5. Boston Consulting Group (2012), *Realizing the Value of People Management*, https://www.bcgperspectives.com/content/articles/people_management_human_resources_leadership_from_capability_to_profitability/.
6. Ibid.
7. Wiley, J. and Kowske, B. (2012), *Respect*. San Francisco, California: Jossey-Bass.
8. www.youtube.com/watch?v=u6XAPnuFjJc (2010).

9. The Economist (2013), Robot Recruiters, How Software Helps Firms Hire Workers More Efficiently, http://www.economist.com/news/business/21575820-how-software-helps-firms-hire-workers-more-efficiently-robot-recruiters.

10. The Economist (2014), The Backlash Against Big Data, http://www.economist.com/blogs/economist-explains/2014/04/economist-explains-10.

11. Knowledge@Wharton (2014), Cade Massey, Managing by The Numbers.

5:   A Toolbox for Managers

1. www.numerology-thenumbersandtheirmeanings.blogspot.com.

2. As mentioned in previous chapters, inspiration for the human capital metrics discussed in this book comes from the set of 200 metrics outlined by the Corporate Leadership Council and InfoHRM in 2005 and the set of 600 metrics outlined and updated by the Human Capital Management Institute in 2013.

3. www.unglobalcompact.org.

4. www.fortune.com/best-companies.

5. Kotter, J. P. (2013), *Management Is (Still) Not Leadership*. Harvard Business Review, https://hbr.org/2013/01/management-is-still-not-leadership/.

6. Ibid.

7. The 70–20–10 training model is accredited to Lombardo and Eichinger (1996).

8. Cascio, W. and Boudreau, J. W. (2011). *Investing in People*. New Jersey: Pearson Education.

6:   Making It Happen

1. SMART versus DUMB targets are illustrated in Chapter 3.

2. Lockwood, N. (2006), Maximizing Human Capital, Society for Human Resource Management, Research Quarterly, http://www.shrm.org/Research/Articles/Documents/0906RQuartpdf.pdf.

3. As an example, the UK Government documented the importance of engaged employees for the British economy and meeting the challenges

of increased global competition in the "Engaging for Success" study by David MacLeod from 2008.

4. Harter, J. and Schmidt, F. (2012), The Relationship Between Engagement at Work and Organizational Outcomes, Q12 Meta-Analysis, http://www.gallup.com/services/177047/q12-meta-analysis.aspx. Q12 meta-analysis initiated by Gallup Q12 is conducted on a regular basis.

5. www.ibm.com, Leadership and Employee Engagement (2014).

6. www.youtube.com, Gary Hamel on the Pyramid of Human Capabilities at Work (2013).

7. Independent research (2008–2013) by Kenexa (now IBM) as well as based on my own measurements at global companies. Confidential data.

7: Limitations and Obstacles

1. http://en.wikipedia.org/wiki/Virtual_team.

2. Attributed to Peter Drucker (2006) in relation with management consultancy to Ford Motor Company. The exact quote cannot be sourced. Peter Drucker was an Austrian-born American management consultant.

3. Kotter, J. P. (1996). *Leading Change*. Boston MA: Harvard Business School.

8: Metrics for Skeptics

1. www.glassdoor.com.

2. en.wikipedia.org/SWOT Analysis.

3. Own survey data on employees experiencing action and behavior change.

4. Psychologist J.P. Guilford developed the concept of divergent thinking in the 1950s. Divergent thinking can be characterized as more open and productive as opposed to convergent thinking which is more closed, mechanical, and looking for one correct answer.

5. Deloitte Consulting (2014), Global Human Capital Trends, http://www2.deloitte.com/global/en/pages/human-capital/articles/human-capital-trends-2014.html.

9:   Calls to Action

1. Inspired by the KIE model by Irmelin Funch Jensen and Ebbe Kromann-Andersen (2009), *Erhvervsskolernes Forlag*, Odense, Denmark.
2. www.tmsworldwide.com (2014), Margerison-McCann Team Management Systems.

Printed and bound by CPI Group (UK) Ltd, Croydon, CR0 4YY